America On The Edge:
Is It Too Late To Turn Back?

By Thomas D. Elliff

NCM PRESS
Oklahoma City, Oklahoma

America On The Edge - Is It Too Late To Turn Back?
First Edition - 1992
Copyright© by NCM Press
2104 Banbury
Oklahoma City, Oklahoma 73170

Unless otherwise stated, all Scripture references in this publication are from the New King James Version, Copyright© 1979, 1980, 1982 by Thomas Nelson, Inc. Used by permission.

Printed in the United States of America
Typesetting - Chris·Malone
Cover Art - BOYDesign
Editor - Don McMinn
Library of Congress Catalog Card Number - 92-61911

ISBN 0-9634614-0-0

Dedicated To
Tom and Gatra Miller
for their constant encouragement
to me in the
Ministry of the Gospel of Christ

Table of Contents

AMERICA ON THE EDGE...

...IS IT TO LATE TO TURN BACK?

FOREWORD

Many years ago, William Booth, the founder of the Salvation Army, described the perilous condition of America in his generation. He said:

1. In America we have religion without the Holy Spirit. Religion is found everywhere, but most of it is without God; it is merely cold, dead, lifeless and dull formalism. Churches are open every Sunday morning but few know anything about the moving of God's Spirit. We have organized and programmed but that is not enough, we must submit to the Holy Spirit.

2. We have Christianity without Christ. Preachers all over America are telling people that there is more than one way to have peace with God, but there is only one way. In John 14:6 Jesus declared *"I am the way, the truth and the life. No one comes to the Father but through me."* Jesus is the only way.

3. We have forgiveness without repentance. Repentance is the forgotten doctrine of the contemporary church, but until we are willing to turn from our wicked ways, God will not prosper our nation.

4. We have politics without God. The Bible declares *"Blessed is the nation whose God is the Lord,"* and if our nation forsakes Him, He will turn His back on us.

5. We have preaching about Heaven without preaching about hell. When was the last time you tuned into a televised worship service and heard the evangelist preach about hell? They don't do it because it doesn't bring the offerings in, people don't like to hear about it, it's not dignified. But during his earthly ministry Jesus said more about hell than he did about Heaven; perhaps because He knew there were more people going to hell than Heaven.

These five problems plagued our nation in Booth's day, and they are about to destroy our nation in this generation.

I remember when President Bush addressed the nation on January 16, 1991 and announced that we were at war. Americans were scared and frightened at the thought of 500,000 of our finest men and women being deployed to foreign soil. The President made two significant statements that evening: He said that we would not require our soldiers to fight with one arm tied behind their back (this was a reference to the bad military policies of the Vietnam War), and secondly he said, **we must pray**. I thought, "Thank God for a President who understands that although we have the best machinery, weapons and manpower of any military complex in the world, if God is not going to fight for us, there is no hope."

And people did pray. The Sunday after war was declared, churches all over America were filled to capacity; prayer meetings were held all over our country.

But less than three weeks after the war was over, a Judge ruled that it was unconstitutional to pray at high-school commencement exercises. Only weeks earlier, our President called our nation to prayer, and God answered, but then a judge declared that by law - you cannot pray. God is not going to be treated like a fire-escape or a spare-tire in the trunk of the car. We cannot just look to Him in times of emergency, we must look to Him all the time.

I have a great concern about who serves in the White House, and about who serves in Congress, but I have an even greater concern for the Judicial branch of our government. It is perhaps the one branch of government that has done the most damage to our country. It was our Supreme Court who ruled that we are no longer allowed to pray at high school commencement exercises, or even pray at football games.

I recently spoke to 6,000 students and parents at South Grand Prairie high school near Dallas, Texas. I was told I could speak on anything I wanted, so I testified about what God had done in my life and about how He got my attention in Vietnam. When I finished speaking, the student body stood to their feet and applauded for four to five minutes. I thought, "When the Supreme Court struck down the privilege to pray in public schools, they were totally out of touch with the morals and desires of grass-roots America." The whole issue of praying at commencement exercises was raised by one junior-high student who said "I don't want prayer at my commencement exercise." In response to this one student, the Supreme Court ruled out prayer, but they have ignored the hundreds of thousands of parents and students who have said

"We don't want humanism and filth pushed down the throats of our young people." The Supreme Court, in the "interest of freedom", eliminated prayer but they allow humanistic teaching.

Yes, the same problems that Booth recognized are rampant today. What can be done to reverse these trends?

I am totally convinced that there is not a man living in America, that could save this nation. I am convinced that if we could find 535 of the most conservative people in our country to serve in the House of Representatives and 100 conservative men and women to serve in the Senate, their influence would still not be enough to turn the heart of our nation. We have only one hope: if the Lord tarries, and if America is to survive, the only hope for our survival is genuine, Holy Ghost, God sent revival. The problem is, most Americans, including many people in our churches, do not have any idea what revival is all about.

What is revival? Charles Finney gave this definition of revival:

"Revival is nothing more than a new beginning of obedience to God. Just in the case of the converted sinner, the first step is deep repentance; a breaking down of the heart, a getting down into the dust before God, with deep humility and a forsaking of sin."

The thought of real revival scares many people because of the changes that it would require, but if revival is our only hope, we should be willing to pay any price.

I've read about the revivals of yesteryear; the revivals of Spurgeon, Whitefield, Moody, Jones, Finney, Wesley and Sunday; but I want to see revival in my generation. I want my children and my grandchildren to be able to say that we had revival in our generation.

And that is why Tom Elliff's new book America On the Edge is so timely and important. It presents the problems, but it also presents the answer. As Christians, we must be knowledgeable on contemporary issues; we need to be able to intelligently refute the drift toward moral decay and defend the timeless truths of God's Word. Pastor Elliff has done our homework for us - his well-documented chapters present a concise but thorough assessment of the problems. This book should incite the conscience of the Christian community and motivate us to action.

Tim Lee - Garland, Texas, September, 1992

# Media/Entertainment

Vladimir K. Zworykin patented the first television tube for Westinghouse in 1923. In 1981 he expressed shock at the worldwide influence of the medium he invented. He commented, "The technique is wonderful. The color and everything are beyond my expectation."

But what did he have to say about the programming that appeared on his invention? "It's awful what they're doing with the subject matter. I would never let my children even come close to this thing."

1

America's Moral Malignancy

"And have no fellowship with the unfruitful works of darkness, but rather expose them. For it is shameful even to speak of those things which are done by them in secret" (Ephesians 5:11-12).

It was the "family hour," and many of America's families sat in front of their television sets watching the premier of a new, highly promoted "family" sitcom. Reviews indicated the program would be both wholesome and hilarious. During the 30 minutes that followed, the teenage star, who had lost her virginity, described the momentous event with vivid expression to her teenaged friend. Subsequently she decided to have an abortion because she was just not "ready to handle the responsibility." Her decision was praised as thoughtful and courageous. The serious nature of immorality and abortion was glossed over by the clever use of comedy.

If the above scene sounds familiar, it is only because it happens all too often in America - so often, in fact, that it is greeted with only nominal protest and wide acclaim. America's entertainment and media industry must bear much of the responsibility for our nation's precipitous moral decline over the last thirty years. It has ceased reflecting the moral values upon which this nation was built, abusing its influence by engaging in a thinly veiled agenda of moral liberality. My heart is filled with righteous indignation as I write to expose the sickening state of morality as expressed by America's media industry. But, according to Paul, I must *"have no fellowship with the unfruitful works of darkness, but rather expose them"* (Ephesians 5:11). As a preacher of the gospel, I am sounding the alarm, alerting you to the evil agenda of this multi-billion dollar industry which, by its own acknowledgment, is no longer seeking to mirror our culture but to mask the wholesome values of the past and move us toward a society as demented and perverted as the lifestyles of the few who control it. Consider the incriminating evidence:

Movies That Sicken

Recently, the motion picture industry bestowed its highest award, "Best Picture Of The Year," to Silence of the Lambs. Movie critic John Evans, in his review of the movie published in Preview, describes the opening scene: A female FBI agent interrogates a prisoner charged with some of the most brutal, cannibalistic types of murders imaginable. As he recounts his heinous crimes, they are vividly portrayed across the motion picture screen. Pictured in this movie, which Hollywood calls "it's best", is a man sewing human skin with a sewing machine, female victims with parts of their skin and fingers missing, a man skinning off the face of a prison guard, a full view of a nude transvestite, seminal fluid being thrown in a woman's face, and dead bodies with their private parts exposed. Throughout the movie, vulgar and offensive language is constantly used.[1] Hollywood's true heart is revealed by its selection of this movie as the best cinematic effort of the year.

This selection shouldn't surprise us, for the year before one of the most highly acclaimed motion pictures was The Cook, the Thief, His Wife, and Her Lover. In Michael Medvid's review of this motion picture, he tells how the movie begins with the brutal beating of an unclothed man while the central figure of the movie stands over him and empties his bladder. The movie ends with the same man slicing a piece of flesh off an elegantly prepared and cooked corpse, making it, as Medvid said, one of the most vivid pictures of cannibalism ever shown. Also featured in this highly acclaimed motion picture were necrophilia (sex with a dead corpse), the bloody and sadistic mutilation of a nine-year-old boy, another victim smeared with human feces, a woman whose face is pierced through with a fork, and two naked bodies writhing in the back of a maggot filled garbage truck.[2]

One would expect Americans to be outraged by the sickening nature of this film. But listen to the media's own assessment of this work: Karen James of The New York Times said, "This motion picture is brilliant." Time Magazine said, "This motion picture was excellent, exciting, and extraordinary."[3] Our nation is morally corrupt.

Many people think they're safe watching the Disney Channel, but consider the moral values of Disney President Jeffrey Kutzenberg. He recently attended a meeting of the Gay and Lesbian Task Force thus offering them his moral support.[4] Or take a few moments to watch "Dinosaurs," the popular television show with subtle innuendos encouraging a homosexual lifestyle. The show's main attraction, a lovable, carnivorous (meat eating) dinosaur family, is surprised to learn that their dinosaur son is a "herbo" who just eats herbs. He is different "by nature," but it's okay. He even frequents a "herbo bar." The program pokes fun at those who believe that homosexuality is wrong, and it encourages openness toward this "alternative lifestyle."[5]

Movie ratings tell the tale of ever increasing moral decline. From 1968-1972, virtually every movie was either rated G or PG. (By the way, movies are rated by the movie industry itself - they decide which movies are "not suitable.") Since 1972 however, the majority of films have either been R-rated or X-rated.[6] For instance, in 1990, of the 570 films produced by the motion picture industry, only eight were for the general audience, 365 were R-rated. That's one R-rated movie a day to stir your sexual appetite but less than one G-rated movie a month to encourage moral values.

Bob DeMoss, youth culture specialist with Focus on the Family, recently interviewed some fourth, fifth, and sixth graders attending a Christian school. One would hopefully have expected from these children more restraint in their television viewing than in the average American home.   DeMoss was shocked however, to discover that some of their favorite movies on television were Nightmare on Elm Street and Friday the Thirteenth. One of the children remarked, "I like how Jason chops people's heads off." Another said, "I like the way people look when they're dead." Still another said, "I like violence and the weapons that they use to kill people."[7] We must not underestimate the powerful influence of the media and entertainment industry on impressionable children, even, much to our sadness, children reared in strong, traditional Christian homes.

Music That Defiles

The music industry also stands charged with encouraging and abetting moral corruption.   The February 1991 issue of "Imprimis," has one   author expressing his distress over the direction the music industry is taking: "The popular music business, for instance, has become a global enterprise of staggering proportions that generates billions of dollars every year through the simple-minded glorification of animal lust."[8] Twenty-four hours a day on MTV, a lifestyle is portrayed that is totally removed from the discipline, the faithfulness, the moral purity, and the integrity one would hope to find in the American family.

Today's rock groups   delight in adopting vile and vividly descriptive names.   Take a quick look at a few names of these popular rock groups:[9]

"Annihilator"	"Coroner"
"Atrocity"	"The Damned"
"Biohazard"	"Dark Angel"
"Carnivore"	"Demolition"

"Clyde Sluts from Hell"	"Devastation"
"Atheist"	"Guillotine"
"Autopsy"	"House of Freaks"
"Black Sabbath"	"Malice"
"Megadeath"	"Violence"
"Morbid Angel"	"The Zombies"
"Obituary"	"Oblivion"
"Onslaught"	"Pestilence"
"Death Angel"	"Slaughter"
"Destruction"	"Social Distortion"
"Entombed"	"Suicidal Tendencies"
"Heathen"	"Torch"
"Legion of Death"	"Venom"
"Massacre"	"Slayer"
"Monstrosity"	"Sodom"
"Napalm Death"	"Thrasher"
"Poison"	"Ultimate Revenge"

Notice the heavy emphasis on death.

It is the cop-out of choice for those who find life too difficult to face. Is there any wonder that suicide now ranks as the second highest cause of death among young people in America?

Some teenagers attempt to minimize the dangerous effect of rock music's foul lyrics by arguing, "It is not the words but the beat that's appealing." But a recent survey taken by the University of Florida indicates that 90% of the teenagers who listen to rock music do know the words, and 60% of them agree with the words. What is most frightening are the main themes of rock music and rap: hatred, domestic violence, child abuse, derision of authority, scorn for education, and the promotion of violence.[10]

Television That Pollutes

Recently, Vice President Dan Quayle was strongly criticized by the news media when he pointed out how the sit-com "Murphy Brown" glamorized the benefits of unwed motherhood. The news media never gave the entire context of his statement. The vice president's premise was that America needs to return to basic family values. He pointed out that among two-parent families, the poverty rate is 5.7%, while among single-parent families it is 33.4%. He underscored his point by saying, "Look, a welfare check is not the same as a father or a husband." But the news media didn't mention this important aspect of his speech. They focused instead on his criticism of "Murphy Brown," one of the media's darlings. Because of this mis-reporting, Quayle received a veritable firestorm of criticism.[11]

"Murphy Brown" is just one of many television celebrities to mock family values. Listen to Barbara, a favorite on "Empty Nest," speak about the archaic tradition of marriage. After making a case for artificial insemination, she asks, "Why should I obligate a man for a whole lifetime when I only need him for an hour?"[12]

An article in TV Guide posed some interesting observations about the morality expressed on some television shows. "Try explaining to your six-year-old, for example, what six-year-old Maizey, on CBS's 'Uncle Buck' means when she tells her brother, 'You suck.' Or what fourteen-year-old Darlene Conner on ABC's 'Rosanne' is talking about when she brags to her sister that she was 'felt up' by her boyfriend."[13]

A recent survey on television violence, commissioned by TV Guide, indicated that in one 18-hour period (6 a.m. - midnight), there were 1,846 individual acts of violence shown on ten channels. Does this violence on television necessarily lead to aggressive behavior in individuals? According to Dr. Leonard D. Eron, the answer is an unqualified yes. Over a period of 22 years, he studied a group of individuals ages 8, 19, and 20. He found that the more television the participants watched at age 8, the more violent their behavior was at age 30. His conclusion: "There can no longer be any doubt that heavy exposure to televised violence is one of the causes of aggressive behavior, crime, and violence in society. The evidence comes from both the laboratory and real-life studies. Television violence affects youngsters of all ages, of both genders, at all socioeconomic levels, and all levels of intelligence."[14]

Network broadcasting is notorious for its tilt to the moral left, usually portrayed in such a subtle manner that it is hard to detect. But the effect, nevertheless, remains.   For instance, the controversy over the abortion pill RU-486 recently came to the forefront of the news because a woman was arrested while bringing the pills into the U.S. from France. The news reports indicated amazement at the Supreme Court's decision refusing to allow her to bring the pills into the U.S. They commented that now the lady would have to have her abortion surgically, since that was the only legal way.   Almost as an aside, the network commentator, with a worried look on his face, told his audience that pharmacists in Europe were greatly afraid of the "radicals" and "fanatics" in America who burn and vandalize abortion clinics. Lacking facts to support that statement, he quickly moved to the next story, leaving the average American with anger in his heart at the pro-life movement. This is media bias in its most insidious but effective form.

Pornography That Corrupts

The most sickening lesion in our moral malignancy is the proliferation of soft and hard core pornography. Pornography is one of the largest industries in our nation - reaping profits in excess of eight billion dollars annually. It has grown from the first Playboy magazine in 1953 to a plethora of magazines, movies and videos which pander to every demon-inspired sexual perversion imaginable.[15]

Pornography is directly linked to many types of violent crimes, most especially those which are sex-related.   The FBI now estimates that over 5,000 murders occur annually because of "recreational killers" who admit that pornography "feeds" their desires.   Additionally, over 1.5 million children are listed as "missing" in America today. Many have been kidnapped and forced to perform unbelievably crude sexual acts.   Under lights and before cameras, some children are tortured and then brutally killed for the production of "snuff films," America's highest priced and most "exotic" type of pornography. The FBI recently broke a crime ring which provides "mail-order children." Their "customers" would simply describe the type of child they wanted and delivery was promised in two weeks.

Forty-one percent of all sex crimes are directly related to the use of pornography. Rape has increased by 700% over the past 30 years and it is estimated that one out of every four young girls who are now under twelve years of age will be sexually assaulted at some time in their life. Ninety percent of child molesters admit they first saw what they did modeled in a pornographic magazine or movie. Many believe that for every reported case of child abuse, nine may go unreported. This means the problem could be ten times larger than statistics reveal.

James Dobson, well-known Christian psychologist, interviewed Ted Bundy only hours before his execution. Bundy killed over two-dozen females in sex-related crimes. He said that his perverted lifestyle began with a seemingly innocent interest in soft core pornography - the kind you see in a pharmacy or grocery store by the cash register. It then progressed from soft-core to hard-core pornography. Ultimately it led him into demonic activity and the brutal slaying of women.

Pornography is now easily accessible in our homes through cablevision. Some people try to justify subscriptions to cablevision with pornographic programming by saying, "Well, I know this is for adults only, but I'm going to monitor it carefully." This is faulty reasoning! Being an adult doesn't make watching pornography any less sinful. Furthermore, when you say "this is for adults only" it only excites the interest of children and intimates that adults are better able to handle perversion than children, which of course, is untrue.

The facts presented above are overwhelming and irrefutable: the media elite and entertainment industries are morally negligent. They have become a malignancy destroying the moral integrity of our nation. In light of these highly disturbing facts, three things are obvious:

I. THERE IS A SINISTER ATTACK ON THE HEART OF AMERICA

The Apostle Paul tells us that, *"For it is shameful even to speak of those things which are done by them in secret"* (Ephesians 5:12). Evidence abounds, some of which is documented below, that there is an agenda by the media elite to transfer those things "done by them in secret" into the soul of our nation.

America was founded upon the principles of the Christian faith. Benjamin Franklin once remarked, "Whosoever will introduce into public affairs the principles of Christianity will change the face of the world." And indeed, Christian principles are at the heart of our nation. But there is an insidious attack on these principles - an overt, aggressive war. And the media and entertainment industry is leading the attack to replace Christian moral values with its own, immoral values. Two pertinent questions arise:

1. Who controls the media and entertainment industries?

In a recent issue of <u>Newsweek</u> magazine, a full page article entitled "The Elite, and How to Avoid It"[17] quoted data gathered by a Washington-based group, "The Center for Media and Public Affairs." Comparisons were made between what those in the media industry think and feel about certain issues and what the average American thinks and feels. A 1991 survey taken among the top leaders of the media industry and from a sampling of "average Americans" reveals some startling differences.

- 85% of Americans still believe that adultery is wrong. Less than 50% of Hollywood executives believe that adultery is wrong.

- Only 4% of Americans have no religious affiliation. Almost 45% of leaders in the media industry have <u>no</u> religious affiliation.

- Over 76% of Americans believe that homosexuality is wrong. Only 20% of Hollywood executives believe that homosexuality is wrong.

- Less than 60% of Americans believe that abortion is right. Almost 97% of Hollywood executives believe that abortion is right.

- A more detailed record of an earlier study by the same group revealed that, of 104 industry executives who were surveyed, only <u>seven</u> said they attended a church regularly. Three-fourths of them admitted they are liberal and lean toward the left.[18]

These Are The People Who Control The Media!

The Scriptures tell us that *"For as he thinks in his heart, so is he"* (Proverbs 23:7). Television programming enters our homes and fills our minds with violence, hatred and sexual immorality, attacking our hearts, seeking our demoralization. When you realize how many hours of television is viewed by the average American each week, is it any wonder that America is in a steep, moral decline?

2. What is the agenda of the Media Elite?

<u>Newsweek</u> columnist Kenneth Woodward states that "There is a genuine culture war going on in American society - in education, the arts, religion, law, politics - and the entertainment media are only its most visible battleground."[19] Or, as Motley Crue says on their album, "Shout at the Devil," "Those who have the youth have the future."[20]

Cal Thomas, noted syndicated commentator, suggests that rock stars can successfully carry out their agenda because they meet at least three basic needs of teenagers - needs which go unmet in most teenager's homes. First, they offer teenagers unlimited time. No rock star ever says, "I don't have time for you now. Come back later." As long as teenagers have time for them, they've got time for teenagers. Second, they offer teenagers complete and unqualified acceptance. "Be as immoral as you want to be and we'll accept you. There is no such thing as "wrong behavior."

Third, they offer teenagers understanding. "We understand the stuff you're going through. We're going through the very same things ourselves."[21] Teenagers, moved by these emotional needs, want to be like rock stars, act like rock stars, and believe what rock stars want them to believe.

The impact of this agenda is reflected in the rising levels of violence. According to the National Family Foundation, "seventy-two percent of junior high school boys want to imitate what they see in sexually oriented, R-rated movies."[22] We cannot help but conclude that there is a sinister attack upon the heart of our nation.

II. THERE IS A SIGNIFICANT AWAKENING IN THE HEART OF AMERICA

Down deep in the heart of most Americans there is a growing and disturbing awareness that something is dreadfully wrong. Most cannot articulate it, but as a society, we are slowly waking up to the sad reality that <u>the media <i>is</i> in the business of mind-control</u> and that <i>the</i> media <u><i>is</i> at war against traditional American values</u> such as work, motherhood, fatherhood, the family, religion, principles, integrity, and ethics. I believe there is a new awakening in America. Americans are saying, "We are sick and tired of this! We want a return to traditional family values!"

Christians in particular find themselves disturbed by the media and entertainment industry because it runs on an opposing course to Scriptural teachings regarding family values. Christians are admonished by the warning in the text, *"Therefore do not be partakers with them. For you were once darkness, but now you are light in the Lord. Walk as children of light (for the fruit of the Spirit is in all goodness, righteousness, and truth...)"* (Ephesians 5:7-9). In today's environment, something so simple as turning on a television set can bring darkness into the family environment.

In recent years, the struggle over which values our nation will embrace has moved into the political arena. Both of America's major political parties placed the issue of "family values on their platforms." While their concept of family values may differ widely from that of the Scripture, the issue of family values *has* become significant. Both parties realize the importance of these key, foundational issues which their candidates ignore only to their peril.

There is an awakening in the heart of America; a deep seated desire to see a return to moral purity, faithfulness in marriage and integrity in the soul.

III. THERE IS A SPIRITUAL ANSWER FOR THE HEART OF AMERICA

Paul reminds us to *"...have no fellowship with the unfruitful works of darkness, but rather expose them...walk circumspectly, not as fools but as wise, redeeming the time, because the days are evil"* (Ephesians 5:11, 15-16). Carefully consider the following:

• **Salvation brings discernment.** Take a hard look at your personal moral commitments and lifestyle. Then settle the issue of your personal salvation. If you have not received Christ as your Savior, you will have no defense against the moral onslaught which assails you. Neither will you be able to adequately protect your family. You will lack discernment, and you will not be able to recognize spiritual darkness. Being morally naive, you'll be easily beguiled by the very industries that seek to destroy your life and your family.

If you have made a commitment to Christ, then you will accept the Bible as the inspired Word of God. It will become your guide for moral decisions. It will be the standard for your home, and in it you will find the principles which will lead you through the waters of moral turbulence.

• **Examine the extent to which you support the media and entertainment industry, either directly or indirectly.** We are encouraged to, *"not be partakers with them...and, have no fellowship with the unfruitful works of darkness"* (Ephesians 5:7-11).

Many people who boast that they do not patronize movie theaters to see indecent pictures will later watch them on television or rent them as a video. This is the ultimate in hypocrisy. It is saying that right and wrong are a matter of geography or witnesses present. We must remember that God is always a witness to our deeds and the intents of our hearts.

Often, a subscription to a cablevision network will provide indirect support for vile, immoral programs, even though you don't allow that programming in your home. Consider your level of participation and remember that it may be costing you something more valuable that money. It could be costing your time, your family, your testimony, or your relationship with God.

● **Stand against evil.** *"Have no fellowship with the unfruitful works of darkness, but rather expose them"* (Ephesians 5:11). Expose the works of darkness. Don't accept excuses like, "If you don't like it, just turn off your TV" or, "if you don't like it, just don't go to those movies." Those statements indicate a basic misunderstanding of the effect of immoral programming.

It affects others than those who choose to support it. If my neighbor starts trashing up his front yard with car parts, I have a legitimate right to complain. If he responds by saying "Just don't look at my trashy yard," that doesn't eliminate the fact that the value of my property is still plummeting; his trash pollutes my environment. Similarly, when the moral environment of my community declines, it affects the value of my family life and the life of every family in my community. So, it is my business.

Standing against evil is every believer's business. I have seen my wife walk into a grocery store, go to the magazine rack, and turn over all the sexually offensive magazines so that only the back covers are visible. I have watched her change the radio tuning in a store from a rock station to a good Christian station. On many occasions she has gone to the manager and asked, "Do you know what's in this magazine? Do you think you should sell this type of material? Would you want your children to see this?" Sometimes there is no change, so we shop elsewhere. If her suggestions are heeded, we keep shopping there. Recently, I told a store manager that a children's book she was selling entitled, <u>Animalia</u>, subtly presents demonism on virtually every page. (Unfortunately, it is a very popular children's book in America today.) She promptly removed the book from the rack, and I have expressed my gratitude to her on subsequent occasions.

- **Do not be intimidated by the cry of "censorship."** You have the right to speak out against what you think is wrong, particularly if you're paying for it! Our government often sponsors and subsidizes art exhibits which are perverted and immoral - all done in the name of "artistic freedom" - at our expense! I am entitled to criticize without hearing someone whine about "unfair censorship." If it's at government expense, I am entitled to be a censor, because I am a sponsor. I should have some input regarding how my tax money is spent. Your opinion is just as valid as the media elite's and you have the right to express it. If you find their work offensive, then say so.

- **Establish standards and policies in your own home.** Establish guidelines relative to the <u>quality</u> of music you will listen to and the type of movies and T.V. programs you will watch. Limit the <u>quantity</u> of time you will allow for media and entertainment. For instance, make a rule that if you watch TV for an hour, you will spend at least an hour talking with your family. Or determine that you will not listen to the bad news on TV unless you have spent at least an hour reading the good news of God's Word.

Revival in the land must start with revival in the family As a family, do your part to stem the tide of moral perversion in our nation and return us to traditional values. Focus upon that which is good, true and pure, and stand against everything that is contrary to the principles of God's Word. There is only one way to deal with a malignancy - it must be removed. Radio, television, the printed page and motion pictures can all be used to bring revival in our land and restoration of moral values; but we must pray for the elimination of twisted thinking on the part of those who control such a key access to the American heart. And we must pray for a return to moral integrity on the part of the both the producers <u>and</u> the participants.

AIDS

"A renowned scientist and developer of the oral polio vaccine, Dr. Albert Sabin, said...he doubts a vaccine can ever be found to halt the spread of the AIDS virus. Writing in the Proceedings of the National Academy of Sciences, Sabin said he is pessimistic because the AIDS virus is transmitted very differently from polio, measles or other diseases whose spread is curbed by vaccine." - From *Wire Services*, September 12, 1992

2

Lust's Epidemic

"But if the watchman sees the sword coming and does not blow the trumpet, and the people are not warned, and the sword comes and takes any person from among them, he is taken away in his iniquity; but his blood I will require at the watchman's hand" (Ezekiel 33:6).

Many of us were riveted to our television screens as a young lady, Kimberly Bergalis, sat in a wheelchair and testified before a special study committee in Washington, D.C. Her body was emaciated; she spoke through clinched teeth, hardly speaking above a whisper. But she was determined to share her message with the world. She had come to Washington with the hope that her testimony would make a difference - Kimberly Bergalis was stricken with AIDS.

Kimberly didn't get AIDS because she was a homosexual, or as a result of sexual promiscuity. She lived a life that was circumspect and above reproach. Kimberly Bergalis was infected by her Florida dentist. Although he knew he had AIDS, he was not required to tell his patients about this fatal, contagious disease.

Before her death, Kimberly Bergalis wrote a letter to the public officials in Florida, holding them responsible for her death because they failed to require her dentist to disclose his AIDS status to his patients.

She said:

I have lived to see my hair fall out, my body lose over 40 pounds and blisters on my sides. I have lived to go through nausea and vomiting, continued night sweats and chronic fevers of 104° that don't go away anymore. I have cramping, diarrhea. I lived to see white fungus grow all over the inside of my mouth, the back of my throat, my gums, and now my lips. I have tiny blisters on my lips that may be the first stages of herpes. Who do I blame? Do I blame myself? I sure don't. I never used I.V. drugs, never slept with anyone, and never had a blood transfusion.

After signing the letter, her post script read:

P.S. If laws are not formed to provide protection, then my suffering and death was in vain. I'm dying guys. Goodbye.[1]

Soon after she delivered her letter, Kimberly Bergalis died, stricken down with AIDS.

What Exactly is AIDS?

AIDS was first diagnosed in 1981 as a disease which attacked the immune system of young homosexual men, causing them to lose their ability to fight off common diseases such as tuberculosis, pneumonia, or even the common cold. Since it initially appeared among young homosexual men, the disease was originally called GRID, Gay Related Immune Deficiency. Later, it was discovered that this tragic disease is no respecter of persons, race, or sex, and that anyone can be infected. The primary characteristic of the virus was the gradual destruction of the immune system, thus the name: AIDS, Acquired Immunodeficiency Syndrome. The virus which produces this syndrome is called HIV, Human Immunodeficiency Virus. Over a period of time it destroys the immune system, crippling a person's ability to resist diseases. The syndrome (AIDS) is the ultimate result of carrying the virus (HIV).[2]

What Does AIDS Do To the Human Body?

When a virus enters the blood stream, a healthy immune system produces antibodies to resist it. A physician diagnoses the virus by observing the presence of antibodies in the blood stream. The insidious nature of the AIDS-producing HIV however, often allows it to go undetected by a blood test for up to three years, although in many cases it may be detected as early as thirty days. The irony is that a person with AIDS can infect others, even though currently testing negative for the virus.

After being infected with HIV, an individual may continue living an apparently normal and healthy life for up to ten years. At some point however, AIDS begins to manifest itself. It destroys the God-given immune system which enables the body to fight off diseases. It is 100% fatal. There is no cure.

When the discussion turns to AIDS patients, we're talking about the very small tip on a very large iceberg, because AIDS is the final stage of the HIV virus. Think of AIDS as the cough that a tuberculosis patient has; it is a symptom of the underlying disease. When you get AIDS, you have about a year and a half to live. In spite of its desire to create no alarm, a government task force on AIDS has admitted that over 80% of the people in America who are infected with AIDS *don't even know it*.[3]

How Do People Get AIDS?

Little is known about the infection process of AIDS. For instance, when a government report states that AIDS cannot be transmitted through a certain process, what they *really* mean is, there is no *recorded* incidence of AIDS being spread in that manner. The brief history of AIDS is filled with facts which reverse previous opinions as to how AIDS can or cannot be transmitted.

Current studies indicate the presence of a new type of AIDS for which there is presently no known method of detection.

Additionally, there are over seven different kinds of AIDS mutations which can infect the body. Many people will die, not of AIDS, but of AIDS-related diseases given to them by people who have AIDS. HIV-infected individuals often develop unique strains of diseases (such as a type of pneumonia) which are highly resistant to antibiotics. When healthy individuals are infected by the new, stronger strain, it becomes exceedingly difficult to treat, causing many people, uninfected by AIDS, to suffer because of those who do.

With the attention of our nation focused upon AIDS, it is imperative for every Bible-believing individual, especially pastors, to cry out against what may be accurately called "lust's epidemic." God spoke to Ezekiel with this solemn admonition: *"If the watchman sees the sword coming, and the people are not warned, his blood I will require at the watchman's hand"* (Ezekiel 33:6). With this Scripture in mind, here are four observations about AIDS.

I. THE REALITY OF AIDS
"If You See Danger..."

In some areas of Africa, one out of every five women who gives birth is HIV positive. Another study indicates that perhaps as many as one out of every three people in the central African nation of Zaire is infected with AIDS. Reports indicate that in some high schools in central Africa, 100% of the students recently tested positive with the HIV virus. Yes, AIDS is a world-wide problem.

Unfortunately, the problem seems far removed when we read statistics about AIDS in other nations. But in America, over a hundred and fifty thousand people have *already* died of AIDS or AIDS-related diseases. The Center for Disease Control says that the death rate will continue to double every thirty months.[4]

Let's consider the dramatic effects when AIDS goes undetected in a community. New York City has over 500,000 people who are HIV positive. Newspapers recently carried the story that on Manhattan Island it is estimated that as many as 25% of all the males under the age of 40 are infected with AIDS.   Chris Norwood, the head of the National Women's Health Network AIDS Committee, says that based on the average number of annual births in New York City, if just 80% of the women in New York City who are already infected, die of AIDS, they will leave between 52,000 and 72,000 orphan children.   Many of these children will also be infected with AIDS. That's not something that *might* happen, that's something that is *going* to happen, ...barring Divine intervention.[5]

The Cost Of AIDS

It is currently estimated that over one and a half million people in the United States have AIDS. Surprisingly, most do not know they have AIDS and may live undiagnosed for up to 10 years. Until then, they may continue to infect others. In your own community, AIDS is taking a tremendous toll creating a dramatic impact on the rising cost of health insurance. In Oklahoma City, Oklahoma, the Occupational Safety and Health Agency has just instigated new AIDS-related protective measures which have increased the cost of ambulance calls by over $30. This increase covers the cost of equipment (goggles, masks, gowns, and shoe coverings) used by paramedics. If, upon inspection, any blood residue is found in an ambulance after it has been prepared for a new call, the company can be fined up to $70,000.

In 1986, the cost of medical care for AIDS patients in the United States, in addition to the lost work force, was a staggering six billion dollars. But by 1991, that cost exceeded $70 billion.[6]

AIDS is a reality. You can say it's not a problem, but it is a problem - in the world, in our nation, in your community, in your home, and in your life. If you decide that you are just not going to worry about it, you're deceiving yourself, because it is a reality - a distressing reality.

II. THE REACTION TO AIDS
"And Do Not Warn The People"

Despite the reality of AIDS, there has been an overwhelmingly irresponsible reaction to AIDS. For instance, on one hand, government agencies are warning all health care personnel to wear double gloves, shoes and gowns in surgery They are told to place shields over their eyes, to breath external air if possible, and use umbrellas when doing any kind of surgery that creates an aerosol effect (spray of blood). Yet on the other hand, they are telling the general public that there is no need for alarm and encouraging them to practice "safe" sex.[7]

Dr. Lorraine Day, a former member of the government AIDS task force, states that AIDS *can* be transmitted by blood through injured skin and that new evidence indicates it may be transmitted through intact skin as well. It can be transmitted pre-natally, that is, from a mother to a child who is still in the womb. It can also be transmitted at birth as the child is coming out of the womb. And although we are told there is no evidence AIDS can be transmitted through urine, body fluids, perspiration, or tears; there is also no evidence that it cannot be transmitted in these ways.[8] Contrary to these facts, the "official word" to the public is that you cannot get AIDS except:

- through direct involvement in sexual contact where body fluids are exchanged,
- through IV drug abuse, blood transfusions,
- prenatally, from an infected mother to her infant,
- through an open wound.[9]

Our Government's Idea Of "SAFE SEX"

But what is the truth about AIDS? The information coming from our government is contradicted by information released from many other credible sources. These differences, if proven accurate, indicate that our U.S. Government's agencies are guilty of a gross misrepresentation on the issue of AIDS. But, by and large, our government has been woefully careless and injudicious in its response to all moral issues. For instance, through the National Endowment of the Arts, we have purveyed pornography to our citizens using taxpayers' money. Some of the most gross, wicked, and vile kinds of displays imaginable are protected under the Freedom of Expression Act. These displays encourage the type of sexual behavior which promotes AIDS.

Look at another example of our government's immoral and hypocritical use of our tax dollars: Since 1988 our government has given in excess of $800,000 to a homosexual organization, the National Association of Black and White Men Together. Almost $200,000 of that money went to sponsor their 1991 convention held in Philadelphia, during which seminars such as "Hot, Horny, and Healthy" were conducted. During one part of the convention participants were encouraged to have "condom races!" - and this at tax payers expense![10] Is this our government's idea of "safe sex?"

Recently, the Oklahoma City chapter of a national homosexual organization called ACT UP distributed an "AIDS Education Packet" to 14- and 15-year-old students on public high school campuses. The contents of these packets encourage perverted sex acts with such instructions as how to cut up latex gloves so they may be used for oral and anal sex. It also lists topics such as: "Masturbating with others is fun, exciting, and safe."[11]

This year our government will spend approximately $450 million funding what they call a "safe sex program," but outside of one man, with one woman, for life, there is no safe sex. The government is acting irresponsibly and is putting vast segments of the population at risk when it condones any type of sexual relationship outside the sanctity of marriage.

The Myth Of "Safe Sex,"
Playing Russian Roulette With Your Life

Incidentally, condoms do not insure "safe" sex. In the article "Condom Roulette" several startling facts are presented which provoke some disturbing questions. Condoms do not create an impenetrable barrier to the transmission of the AIDS virus. First of all, condoms are only effective as a contraceptive 84.3% of the time. Sperm will pass through a condom 15.7% of the time. Since a woman is only fertile a few days of each month, the chances of becoming pregnant are diminished. However, the AIDS virus is 450 times smaller than sperm, so the effectiveness of condoms as a barrier is much less than 84.3%. In addition, you must realize that AIDS can be contracted every day of the month. Do you want to risk your life on those odds?

Suppose you are a parent and your son wants to play high school football. You're asked to sign a medical permission slip that says, "In any given year, out of the twenty-two boys on the team, at least three of them will have a fatal accident on the football field." Are you going to sign that permission slip? That's the same chances a person has of getting AIDS through what's called "safe sex." Or suppose you join a skydiving club with five others. Before you go up for your first jump, the instructor says that every year for the past ten years, one group member's parachute has failed to open. Are you going to participate in the jump?[12]

Magic Johnson's "Safe Sex" Stand
Proves Disappointing

Most of us, at one time, have been fans of Magic Johnson. When he first admitted to having AIDS, he said he was going to help the government promote "safe sex." The folly of this strategy is spelled out in a letter written by Robert Lewis, pastor of

Fellowship Bible Church in Little Rock, Arkansas, to Magic Johnson:[13]

Dear "Magic" Johnson,

You don't know me, but I've been a fan of yours for years. No one in basketball has ever done better than you, Magic. The Magic man is a nickname you truly deserve.

Hearing you have the HIV virus took my breath away. I was stunned and shocked. I appreciated the bravery you exhibited in making your illness known. Since I know what is ahead of you first hand (my brother died of AIDS last August), I felt your pain all the more.

Nevertheless, your public statement left me uneasy. Forgive me for saying this, but for some reason, I felt like you were still playing to the crowd when you offered yourself as a safe sex advocate. Certainly, this will play well to the liberal media, special interest groups, AIDS activists, Planned Parenthood, and the like. They will exalt your every move.

But, somehow, from a hero, I expected more. I wanted to hear Ervin share his heart, not Magic play the crowd. I wanted tears, not that big smile. I wanted to hear you say that you were deceived, that life was more than a game. I wanted you to tell young people, my kids especially, that you regret the hundreds of women you used as playthings and sex objects and who in turn used you. But instead, my boys heard you say that it's OK to use women, just be safe. For my daughters, I wanted you to apologize to the many you, no doubt, gave the AIDS virus to. They're going to die, Ervin. I wanted to hear you say that you wished you had married your high school sweetheart sooner and that a lifelong commitment is better than indiscriminate pleasures. I would like to have seen you cry for the child your wife bears who won't have a daddy to grow up with. I would like to have heard you admit what our nation is forever denying: that we live in a moral universe with moral absolutes that sooner or later will judge those who break them.

Instead, you have chosen to become a "safe sex" spokesman. You're going to tell kids to do something you never did. What's worse, it's not safe. Hasn't anyone ever told you, Ervin, that a condom doesn't always work, that it will fail the

user a certain percentage of the times, that your playing HIV
roulette? Years from now, hasn't it occurred to you that there
will be a number of boys and girls, adults then, hospitalized with
bleeding, cancerous sores, dripping on their sheepskin mats with
TB in their intestines, pneumonia covering their lungs and tubes
running out of every conceivable place, blind in both eyes, with
a ventilator forcing oxygen into their now shrunken, disease
ridden bodies, prolonged only with the agony and torture, and
they will be saying "Magic told us it was safe." But by then,
you will have passed the ball to someone else. They'll be left to
discover the awful truth for themselves that Ervin's magic
worked on a basketball court where he lived by rules and not off
the court where he didn't live by rules.[14]

So by promoting "safe sex" and issuing conflicting information,
our government is responding to the AIDS crisis in a careless and
fraudulent manner.[15]

Special Interest Groups
Push Their Own Agenda

Certain special interest groups have proven to be particularly
irresponsible regarding the AIDS crisis, especially homosexual
groups. It is disturbing to see politicians capitulating to their
demands for legislation, protecting homosexuals as a minority
group. They should no more be protected under that designation
than the mafia. (And their behavior kills more people.) A
homosexual is a person who has made a *behavioral* choice. While
all of us are born with a sin nature, that does not give us license
to act irresponsibly. You cannot be a former Hispanic or a
former Black, but you can be a former homosexual.[16]

Some public figures have indicated that the homosexual
community is responding properly to the AIDS crisis because
reported cases of AIDS are declining among homosexuals.
However, one must search for the real cause of this decline. In
reality, they are simply running out of people to infect.[17] In 1978,
6,800 homosexuals in San Francisco participated in a special blood
test, because homosexuals have a high incidence of the Hepatitis

B virus. These formed a base line to measure the AIDS infection. After the tests were performed, their blood serum was saved. Their 1978 blood serum had a 3% AIDS infection rate. In 1981, they retested the same group of people and 36% of them had AIDS. Today, 80% of them test positive for AIDS. In other words, this homosexual test group has rapidly increased its AIDS infection rate and is dying off. The test group has become smaller, making it appear that AIDS is on the decline. As time passes, this percentage will get even smaller - but not because they are acting responsibly.

These special interest groups are also conveying misleading information about sex and AIDS. Debrah Hafner writes and speaks for SIECUS, Sex Information Education Council of the United States. This organization has a profound effect on much of the sex education materials that children receive and use in public schools. Speakers from SIECUS are invited by many public schools across the nation to share in their sexual awareness conferences. Here's a typical statement from Debrah Hafner: "Flirting, dancing, undressing each other, masturbation alone, with a partner, or mutual masturbation, you come up with your own list of safe activities."[18] Has SIECUS been to your neighborhood school? Would you want your children exposed to this kind of "safe sex" education?

Additionally, the media also shares guilt in undermining the moral fiber of our country by encouraging sexual promiscuity. Every year on public television there are 20,000 acts of implied intercourse; and it's even more common on cablevision. This past year virtually every mid-adolescent female television star was portrayed as losing her virginity during the course of the program.

III. DIVINE RETRIBUTION
"They Shall Die In Their Sins..."

Sin <u>always</u> results in judgment. AIDS is one of God's judgments of a sinful and perverted society. *"For he who sows to his flesh will of the flesh reap corruption"* (Galatians 6:8). Note that although AIDS initially appeared among those who gave themselves to sexual promiscuity, innocent people are eventually adversely affected (Daniel loved God with all of his heart, but he was in captivity all of his life because of the sins of his forefathers).

Many people find it repugnant to think of God bringing such severe judgment on sin. In reality, just as AIDS cripples the immune system of the body, sin cripples the health of any society. Our society is now reaping God's judgment, as spoken of in the first chapter of Romans, *"Therefore God also gave them up to uncleanness, in the lusts of their hearts... (vs.24) God gave them up to vile passions... (vs. 26) God gave them over to a debased mind... (vs. 28)"*

What happens when God gives up on someone? It means that the Holy Spirit no longer actively works within that person to convict him of sin and righteousness and judgment. The person is able to do what he wants without any fear of divine retribution.

Likewise, God's greatest judgment of our nation is for Him to give us up to our sinful way. That is, He allows us to continue in sin, offering no "immune system," which in essence is a case of "social" AIDS - a deficiency in our capacity to detect and battle against sins. Yes, AIDS is an evidence of divine retribution.

IV. THE DETERMINED RESPONSE
"And warn them..."

The Lord says, *"I have no pleasure in the death of the wicked, but that the wicked turn from his ways and live. Turn, turn, from your evil ways! For why should you die"* (Ezekiel 33:11). Can we be delivered? Following are six essential steps in turning from our evil ways, that we might receive deliverance from the Lord.

- Trust in Jesus as your personal Savior. Only through His grace and power can you be delivered from sin and have power over sin. Furthermore, when you receive Christ as your Savior, the Bible becomes a living book which can guide your life and your family.

- Make a commitment of your life to practice moral purity. There is no such thing as being "sort of" pure. Purpose in your heart that you will live by the standards clearly outlined in Scripture.

- Make a commitment to raise up a Godly heritage. Parents, it's one thing to give a lecture; it's another thing to live an exemplary life. You cannot raise up a Godly heritage with the T.V. running all the time, the radio blaring, your Bible never opened, and poor church attendance. If you don't live a life that is above reproach, you can't expect your children to do more. You will not lecture them into purity; they learn how to make decisions by seeing how you make your decisions. It's not easy to raise up a Godly heritage; it takes work. It may require many agonizing nights on your knees. But it is possible.

- You must speak against sin. Call sin what it is and seek to deliver the sinner. God hates sin - God loves sinners. When Jesus ministered to the Samaritan woman, He denounced the sin that was in her life, but He loved her and delivered her from her sin. Sometimes it's easier to get on a band wagon and denounce AIDS than it is to share your faith. If you're going to preach against AIDS, you must preach for Jesus. If you're going to tell people they are going to die with AIDS and go to Hell without Christ, you'd better also tell them how they can go to Heaven through faith in Christ instead, even though they have a fatal disease.

- You must join with your church in reaching out to victims of AIDS and their families. Often, when people get a terminal disease, people treat them like they are not "real" people. They are real people, and they are hurting. We need to reach out with compassion.

- You must pray a prayer of repentance for the sins of our nation. Repent of your own sin of lack of concern and involvement. Seek the face of God. God says... *"Then I will hear from Heaven, and will forgive their sin and heal their land..."* of AIDS:Lust's Epidemic.

Abortion

A Summary of the Case, Jane Roe versus Henry Wade
Argued December 13, 1971. Reargued October 11, 1972.
Decided January 22, 1973.

An unmarried pregnant woman who wished to terminate her pregnancy by abortion instituted an action in the United States District Court for the Northern District of Texas, seeking a declaratory judgment that the Texas criminal abortion statutes, which prohibited abortions except with respect to those procured or attempted by medical advice for the purpose of saving the life of the mother, were unconstitutional. She also sought an injunction against their continued enforcement. A physician, who alleged that he had been previously arrested for violations of the Texas statues and that two prosecutions were presently pending against him in the states courts, sought and was granted permission to intervene. All parties took protective appeals to the United States Court of Appeals for the Fifth Circuit, which court ordered the appeals held in abeyance pending decision on the appeal taken by all parties to the United States Supreme Court, from the District Court's denial of injunctive relief.

On appeal, the United States Supreme Court reversed the district Court's judgment as to the physician-intervenor, dismissing his complaint in intervention, but affirmed the District Court's judgment in all other respects. In an opinion by Blackmun, J., expressing the views of seven members of the court, it was held that (1) the pregnant, unmarried woman had standing to sue, (2) the complaint of the childless, married couple presented no actual justiciable case or controversy and had been properly dismissed, (3) states have legitimate interests in seeing to it that abortions are performed under circumstances that insure maximum safety for the patient, (4) the right to privacy encompasses a woman's decision whether or not to terminate her pregnancy, (5) a woman's right to terminate her pregnancy is not absolute and may to some extent be limited by the state's legitimate interests in safeguarding the woman's health, in maintaining proper medical standards, and in protecting potential human life, (6) the unborn are not included within the definition of "person" as used in the Fourteenth Amendment, (7) prior to the end of the first trimester of pregnancy, the state may not interfere with or regulate an attending physician's decision, reached in consultation with his patient, that the patient's pregnancy should be terminated, (8) from and after the end of the first trimester, and until the point in time when the fetus becomes viable, the state may regulate the abortion procedure only to the extent that such regulation relates to the preservation and protection of maternal health, (9) from and after the point in time when the fetus becomes viable, the state may prohibit abortions, altogether, except those necessary to preserve the life or health of the mother, and (10) the state may proscribe the performance of all abortions except those performed by physicians currently licensed by the state; and expressing the view of six members of the court, it was held that the physician's complaint should be dismissed and he should be remitted to his remedies in the pending state court proceedings.

3

When America Sold Its Soul To Satan

"Deliver those who are drawn toward death,
And hold back those stumbling to the slaughter. If you
say, 'Surely we did not know this,' Does not He who
weighs the hearts consider it? He who keeps your soul,
does He not know it? And will He not render to each
man according to his deeds" (Proverbs 24:11-12)?

On January 22, 1973, a great, dark, bloody stain appeared on the soul of our nation. On that day America, which for decades had been sliding down the slippery slope of immorality, finally sold its soul to the devil. On that day the Supreme Court, in the case Roe versus Wade, rendered a decision that protected the murderer and ignored the helpless victim. On that day the Supreme Court of our land legalized abortion.

Prior to 1973 the fact that all men are created with certain inalienable rights, including the right to life, was one of the most cherished tenets in the soul of our nation. But when that principle was torn from our heart, it began a hemorrhage of ever-increasing proportion. Subsequent to the Roe versus Wade decision:

- **A minor no longer must receive parental consent to have an abortion.** A minor who cannot be given an aspirin at school can consult a school counselor, the counselor can refer her to Planned Parenthood, and Planned Parenthood, if counsel deems it advisable, can recommend and arrange an abortion without her parent's knowledge.

- **Late term abortions are allowed.** Abortions can be performed even during the third trimester of pregnancy. This means that a child who could survive outside the womb may be killed inside the womb.

- **Our tax dollars now subsidize abortions.** In many cases, counseling organizations which are pro-abortion receive funding from national or state tax revenues. In some states, welfare recipients can receive state aid for abortions.

- **Massive advertisement is used by abortion clinics.** The availability of an abortionist and the convenience of getting an abortion has greatly increased. Business is so good that many abortion clinics advertise out of state with toll-free numbers.

- **Abortion has now become the contraceptive of choice for many women.** In over ninety percent of cases, "unwanted pregnancy" is stated as the reason for abortion. Forty percent of abortions are repeat abortions and many women have up to five abortions.

We shudder at the biblical account of heathen religions and their practice of human sacrifice. For instance, as a part of the worship of Molech, a Canaanite god, the inside of a great brass idol would be heated until the arms glowed and became searing hot. Parents would place their children in the burning hands of Molech and watch them die. This ancient practice seems so barbaric and inhumane, but now parents allow money-motivated abortionists to place their hands on their children and sacrifice them on the godless altar of Satanically-inspired secular humanism.

Every true believer in Christ must consider at least three issues relative to abortion:

I. HAVE WE REALLY ACKNOWLEDGED THE SIN OF ABORTION?

Proverbs 24:11 says, *"deliver those who are drawn toward death."* If we plead ignorance of this horrible sin, we will come under the judgment of the One who weighs our hearts, keeps our souls, and renders to each of us according to our work.

Abortion Is Real In America

Many Americans, including many believers, do not fully understand the significance of the abortion problem. It may not have touched your home, but it has touched our nation. Since January 22, 1973, the daily rate of abortions has progressively increased to where now over 4,000 are performed each day. It is realistically estimated that over 26,000,000 babies have been killed at the hands of abortionists in the last 20 years.

The most common argument used by the pro-abortionist is that this practice protects the health and life of mothers. But in the year preceding Roe versus Wade (1972) the U.S. Center for Disease Control recorded that approximately 39 women had died as a result of back-alley abortions.[1] Now medical experts admit in frustration, that annually more women than that die or experience severe complications from the procedures used in abortion clinics. One employee of an abortion clinic admitted that during the removal of a baby by suction it is possible for a woman's intestines to be sucked through the uterus and out the cervix. And since many abortion clinics discourage the presence of ambulances, women who are injured during their abortion are often hurried out the back door, placed in a car, and rushed to the emergency room of a nearby hospital.[2] Death is the product of abortion, <u>always</u> for the child and <u>sometimes</u> for the mother.

It is a sad truth, America sold its soul to the devil - for money, convenience and the propagation of an immoral lifestyle.

- **For money** - Abortion is a multi-billion dollar operation. Carol Everett, in her book <u>The</u> <u>Scarlet</u> <u>Lady</u>, states that in her previous association with an abortion clinic, she was making more than ten thousand dollars per month.[3]

- **For convenience** - Parents often encourage their daughter to have an abortion because her pregnancy would be inconvenient for both them and her. A man who discovers his partner is pregnant often encourages her to have an abortion because he doesn't want the responsibility of fatherhood or limitations on his sexual activities. Pregnant women will sometimes choose an abortion because they have too many children already; it's just more convenient to kill the one they can't see.

- **For immorality** - We are constantly shocked by the statistics that reveal the number of people involved in sexual intercourse outside of marriage. The legalization of abortion provided a simple way to remove the unwanted consequences of an immoral lifestyle.

Abortion is real in America...and it is a sin.

Abortion Is Repugnant To God

God hates murder. *"You shall not murder"* (Exodus 20:13). God especially hates the murder of those who are absolutely innocent and totally defenseless. An abortionist preys upon innocent people, much like the Amalekites did in Bible times. The Amalekites attacked the children of Israel after they came out of the land of Egypt. As the Israelites marched through the wilderness, the Amalekites would find those who were weak, pregnant, old, helpless and defenseless and prey upon them. God said the world could not tolerate the Amalekites and commanded that the entire nation be exterminated.

God considers an unborn baby a real person. Psalm 139:13-16 tells us that a child is known by God even before it is developed in the mother's womb.

> *"For You have formed my inward parts; You have covered me in my mother's womb. I will praise You, for I am fearfully and wonderfully made; marvelous are Your works, and that my soul knows very well. My frame was not hidden from You, when I was made in secret, and skillfully wrought in the lowest parts of the earth. Your eyes saw my substance, being yet unformed. And in Your book they all were written, the days fashioned for me, when as yet there was none of them."*

Furthermore, according to Levitical law, a child in its mother's womb was to be protected as a human being. The consequences for killing a baby in its mother's womb, even in the case of an accident, were severe.

> *"If men fight, and hurt a woman with child, so that she gives birth prematurely, yet no lasting harm follows, he shall surely be punished accordingly as the woman's husband imposes on him"* *(Exodus 21:22).*

Abortion is repugnant to God.

Abortion Requires A Response From God's People

Silence on moral issues is not an option for the Christian. We must respond. Read Proverbs 24:12 again and note that God will hold us accountable for our response to this moral dilemma. Silence brings judgment.

We would do well to remember the experience of Dietrich Bonhoeffer. From his prison cell, Bonhoeffer recalled his silence when the Nazis came for the Jews, herded them onto cattle cars, and shipped them to concentration camps. When they arrived to arrest Bonhoeffer, there was no one left to speak on his behalf; they had all gone before him. I repeat, silence is not an option.

II. ARE WE REALLY ANGUISHING OVER THE SIN OF ABORTION?

The acknowledgment that innocent children are being drawn to death must be accompanied with great anguish of soul over their plight. *"Oh hold them back!"* pleads the writer of Proverbs. This statement implies that your concern must be born from an anguished heart.

One reason Americans are not bothered by abortion is that we have been emotionally desensitized. We are lulled to sleep each evening listening to the ten o'clock news report of the latest death count, the latest war, the latest crime.

In the August 17, 1992 edition of <u>Newsweek</u> magazine, it was noted that on a random day (April 2, 1992) in one city (Washington), researchers counted 1,846 acts of TV violence. Children's cartoons were the most violent type of show, followed by movies, toy commercials and music videos.[4]

When we become accustomed to seeing brutality, life becomes cheap and we get desensitized. We begin to think of people as something other than human beings.

There are specific matters which should pierce your heart and produce anguish.

The Plight Of The Innocent, Defenseless Child - The Victim

We should cry out to God on behalf of these children. Nationally known radio teacher, David Hocking, in his outstanding book <u>The Moral Catastrophe</u>, lists the six most prevalent ways children are aborted. Let me summarize them for you in chronological sequence, depending on the stage of the pregnancy.

- In the early stages of pregnancy, the abortionist uses a suction curettage or dilation curettage. In this procedure, a loop-shaped knife is put up through the cervix and into the womb. By means of a suction tube the child is systematically dismembered, and the parts are sucked into a jar.

- From the fourth month, an abortionist often uses an intercardial injection. A needle is inserted through the women's abdomen, through the amniotic cavity, and into the beating heart of the child. The baby is then given a lethal injection. The child dies immediately and is later aborted by the mother.

- From four to six months, the dilation and evacuation technique is used. Forceps with sharp teeth are placed through the cervix and into the womb, grasping the baby's arms and legs and twisting them off. Then the forceps are put around the head of the child (sometimes the child is still alive); the skull and spine are crushed and then removed. Tragically, sometimes the abortionist does not remove all the parts. There are accounts of distressed women returning to the clinic because there is still a foot, arm, or leg inside the womb.

- From four to seven months, a saline solution is often used. A lethal solution is injected into the amniotic fluid, the child breathes it and begins to die. The saline solution sears the skin of the child. Within twenty-four hours the delivery usually occurs, but the child is not always dead when born.

- From four to eight months, the abortionist often uses a substance called prostaglandin, a hormone-like substance which causes the mother to begin her contractions and deliver the child. This procedure is complicated by occasional live births in addition to physical problems to the mother.

- From four months to full term, a C-section is commonly used. In this technique, the womb of the mother is sliced open; and the doctor does one of two things with the baby. He may reach into the mother's womb and strangle the baby, or he make take it out and set it aside so that it will die of neglect.[5]

How can we not anguish over the plight of the innocent child?

The Perverted Sense Of Morality Expressed By - The Abortionist

Recently, in Oklahoma City, often called the "buckle" of the Bible Belt, an abortionist lost the lease on his office building because of an unusual turn of events - the air-conditioning repairman found the attic filled with jars holding the bodies of babies. It was later discovered that periodically the bodies were removed from the attic, dumped in a pile, and incinerated in a field. An outraged community, horrified by the discovery of a pile of bodies not totally burned, demanded action against the physician. When called to appear before the medical board to give an account of his practice, he explained that his religion did not allow the burial of people but did allow for cremation. The irony is, *by his own testimony*, he was admitting that unborn babies are indeed human beings. The medical board could not arrive at a majority decision to revoke his license or censure him. It was a heinous, irresponsible act on the part of the physician and the medical board.

Why should we have anguish in our hearts for the abortionist? Can you imagine the guilt and confusion that an abortionist must have as he becomes aware that on the other end of the forceps there is a life and death struggle. And what about the seared conscience of the woman who joked about how many hands and feet go down the garbage grinder of her husband's abortion clinic?[6]

Several years ago I had the privilege of leading to Christ a physician who had performed many abortions. In tears he related that the only hope he ever had of seeing those children and asking their forgiveness was to see them in Heaven.

We should pray that the abortionists will turn from their heinous crimes, for one day they must stand before a holy and righteous God who will mete out perfect justice.

The Perpetrators Of Abortion - The Parents

Think for a moment about the father of aborted children. If he encouraged the abortion, he is not only an accomplice to murder, but he is exhibiting gross insensitivity to the child's mother. Perhaps he thinks the abortion will allow him to continue a normal relationship with the mother. In reality, only two out of eleven relationships are still in place within seven months after the abortion they sought for the "good" of their relationship.[7]

And what about the mother who agrees to the abortion? Ninety percent experience some kind of clinical, emotional depression after the abortion.[8] This in addition to the agony experienced during the abortion. Nancy Mann, in her book <u>When Does Life Begin?</u>, tells her own story about the trauma of having an abortion:

>"After the fluid was withdrawn, he injected 200cc's of the saline solution - half a pint of concentrated salt solution. From then on it was terrible.

>My baby began thrashing about - it was like a boxing match. She was in pain. The saline was burning her skin, her eyes, her throat. It was choking her, making her sick. She was in agony, trying to escape.

>For some reason it had never entered my mind that with an abortion she would have to die. I had never wanted my baby to die; I only wanted to get rid of my "problem."

>But it was too late to turn back now. There was no way to save her. So instead, I talked to her. I tried to comfort her. I tried to ease her pain. I told her I didn't want to do this to her, but it was too late to stop it. I didn't want her to die. I begged

her not to die. I told her I was sorry, to forgive me, that I was wrong, that I didn't want to kill her. For two hours I could feel her struggling inside me.

But then, as suddenly as it began, she stopped. Even today, I remember her very last kick on my left side. She had no strength left. She gave up and died.

Despite my grief and guilt, I was relieved that her pain was finally over. But I was never the same again. The abortion killed not only my daughter, it killed a part of me.

A little while after my baby stopped moving they gave me an intravenous injection to help stimulate labor. I was in hard labor for 12 hours, all through the night. When I finally delivered, the nurses didn't make it into my room in time.

I delivered my daughter myself at 5:30 the next morning, October 31. After I delivered her, I held her in my hands. I looked her over from top to bottom. She had a head of hair, and her eyes were open. I looked at her little tiny feet and hands. Her fingers and toes even had swirls of fingerprints. Everything was perfect. She was not a fetus. She was not "a product of conception." She was a tiny human being...she was my daughter. Twisted with agony, silent and still. Dead.

Several months later, at 22 years of age, I was forced to undergo a total hysterectomy - all because of that safe and easy, legal abortion.[9]

In our outraged state of moral indignation, we are often moved to pray "against" the abortionist and those who choose to have one. But in our response we must have Christlike love and concern for the people involved, while hating the sin.

III. HAVE WE TAKEN THE PROPER ACTION REGARDING THE SIN OF ABORTION?

If we acknowledge that abortion is sin and if we anguish over its results, we will be motivated to action. Proverbs says, *"Deliver those who are drawn toward death, and hold back those stumbling to the slaughter."* What kind of action can we take?

- **Pray.** Weep before God over the soul of this nation and over the hard-heartedness that would allow this travesty to flourish. We must pray that God would reverse it. We must pray that America will find itself once again moving toward God, not running away from Him. The hard truth is that moral reformation will never take place in our land apart from personal spiritual revival. Pray for revival in the land.

- **Get informed.** Become acquainted with the laws and your law-makers. What is your state's legal position on abortion? What current legislation is before the courts? Where do your elected officials stand on this issue? Call and write your elected officials, ask probing questions, and do not fear informing them of your position.

- **Get involved.** Support crisis pregnancy centers and counseling and adoption agencies. If you choose to demonstrate at pro-life rallies, make sure the manner of your demonstration does not breach laws and create a situation where your good can be spoken of as evil. Vote - sixty percent of Americans do not vote on a regular basis. Support political candidates who are pro-life. Find out what your local schools are teaching children about sex. Are they advocating abortion as a viable alternative to an unwanted pregnancy?

- **Be prepared to adequately and accurately speak on your pro-life stance.** Pro-choice advocates must hear the truth (not supposition) intelligently expressed. In a recent issue of <u>Citizen</u> published by James Dobson's "Focus On The Family," several questions were listed that could be asked of pro-choice advocates. Here is a summary of several of those questions.

    ▸ "Does someone's right to privacy exceed one's right to live?"

▶ "If women are really supposed to control their own
   bodies, then why can't they control their own bodies
   regarding drugs or immorality?"

▶ "Why do people who say that there should be no
   government interference also say that they should get
   government subsidy?"

▶ "If helping women is really the only goal of an
   abortion clinic, then what are you doing to help any
   women besides killing her child?"

▶ "If absence of a heartbeat means a person is dead, then
   why doesn't the presence of a heartbeat mean a person
   is alive?"

▶ "When an unborn child is treated in its mother's
   womb, who is the patient?"

▶ "If you're so concerned with health and health
   standards, why do you fight against any legislation
   which requires that an abortion clinic meet the same
   standards as a hospital?"

▶ "Let's both of us examine the down side of our
   position. Let's both suppose we're wrong. Who
   comes out the winner?"[10]

Yes, on January 22, 1973, America sold its soul to Satan.
God has spoken clearly on this issue; He sets Himself against
people who take other's lives needlessly. He brings destruction to
nations that condone murder of the innocent and helpless. America
is not on good ground with God. We cannot shake our fists in the
face of a holy God who says *"Thou shalt not kill,"* continue to
commit 4,000 murders a day, and not expect to face the
consequences.

We must deliver those who are being taken away to death.

Prayer in School

A Summary of the Case, Steven Engel versus William Vitale
Argued April 3, 1962. Decided June 25, 1962.

The state of New York adopted a program of daily classroom prayers in public schools; the prayer in question was brief, denominationally neutral, and its observance on the part of the students was voluntary. Shortly after the adoption of the program, the parents of ten pupils brought the present action in mandamus in the New York Supreme Court, Nassau County, challenging the constitutionality of both the state law authorizing the school district to direct the use of the prayer in public schools and the school district's regulation ordering the recitation of the prayer on the ground that these actions violated that part of the First Amendment which commands that Congress shall make no law respecting an establishment of religion. The request for mandamus was denied by the trial court, but the matter was remanded to the Board of Regents for adjusting its regulations with a view to protecting voluntariness of participation in the prayer. The Appellate Division affirmed. The Court of Appeals likewise affirmed the order below.

On certiorari, the United States Supreme Court reversed. In an opinion by Black, J., expressing the view of five members of the Court it was held that by using its public school system to encourage recitation of the prayer, the state of New York adopted a practice wholly inconsistent with the clause of the First Amendment, applicable to the states by virtue of the Fourteenth Amendment, which prohibits laws respecting an establishment of religion.

4

When America Began
To Self-Destruct

Deuteronomy 6:12-15 is the story of our nation:

"Beware, lest you forget the Lord who brought you out of the land of Egypt, from the house of bondage. You shall fear the Lord your God and serve Him, and shall take oaths in His name. You shall not go after other gods, the gods of the peoples who are all around you (for the Lord your God is a jealous God among you), lest the anger of the Lord your God be aroused against you and destroy you from the face of the earth."

June 25, 1962, marked a major turning point in the history of America. On that day the United States Supreme Court, in the case Engel versus Vitale, ruled to limit the practice of prayer in public schools.[1] Why did this happen in America? When did the moral tide peak, then slowly ebb out? Where did we lose our valued sense of faith in God? Along what road did we turn aside from the basic idea that our government would not, indeed, could not work unless its people were willing to submit to the higher authority of God?

What can a nation expect when it steps away from God's protection? God reminded the children of Israel that the failure to fear and serve Him would cause *"...the anger of the Lord your God be aroused against you and destroy you from the face of the earth"* (Deuteronomy 6:15). Should America, supposedly "one nation under God," be required to love Him any less than Israel? And should our failure to do so result in any lesser judgment than that promised to the children of Israel?

Let's take a look at our historical roots and note when we began to drift from our moral moorings.

I. THERE IS A PRINCIPLE WHICH DISTINGUISHES THE HERITAGE OF OUR NATION

America's history is unique among all the other nations of the modern world. (This statement evokes an unpopular sentiment in a generation which hears much about a "global community" that will supposedly break down all political barriers and make us not Americans but "citizens of the world." In reality, globalism is simply a part of Satan's plot to move the world toward his "one-world government.") There is something unique about the conception of our nation, and this uniqueness has been the foundational building block of our country.

From its inception, our nation's government has been based upon two major tenets: 1) the acknowledgement of a Sovereign God, and 2) man's responsibility before God. These two principles are so tightly woven into the fabric of our republic that their removal would destroy its capacity to function properly. Our government must operate on the principle that God is the ultimate authority and that all men, including our national leadership, are ultimately accountable to Him. These two principles bring to every citizen an appeal for discipline, respect, and Godly self-rule.

But starting in the mid-50's, many of our nation's progressive, reform-minded educators began a reinterpretation of American history. Under the guise of "de-bunking" American history, they allowed their own, self-centered morality to alter their concepts on history. This resulted in a historical perspective which was designed to defend their own lack of faith and condone their own poor moral behavior.

I was in high school and college during the late 50's and early 60's and saw these subtle shifts taking place. At first the strategy was to denounce our nation's "heroes." Our founding fathers, who had espoused great values and ideals, were portrayed as nothing more than greedy, grasping, capitalistic, imperialistic individuals. While no one can overlook the errors of faith and behavior in the life of any group of men, including our founding fathers, there is at the same time, conclusive evidence that many of America's founding fathers did have noble, heroic, Godly qualities and motives.

For instance, we recently celebrated the five-hundred-year anniversary of Christopher Columbus' "discovery" of America. Before and during the celebration, there was an attempt to portray Columbus as a greedy man who had no thought of God. Some even questioned the validity of his role in our nation's history. It appeared that there was deliberate intention to do away with Columbus Day. Regardless of who is ultimately proven to be the "discoverer of America," Columbus did seek the Lord, and his motivation for exploration was biblical. Here is an excerpt from his diary:

> "It was the Lord who put it in my mind. I could feel His hand upon me. There is no question that the inspiration was from the Holy Spirit because He comforted me with rays of illumination from the Holy Scriptures. It was simply a fulfillment of what Isaiah had prophesied--the fact that the Gospel must be preached to so many lands. No one should fear to undertake a task in the name of the Savior if it is just and if the intention is purely for His service and His alone."

Students in our classrooms saw a switch from an emphasis upon the noble qualities of our founding fathers to an emphasis on the sin in their lives. Suddenly, the historical fabric of America began to unravel; we lost our heroes; we became disenchanted with our cultural heritage, and expressions of national pride were considered naive. We lost the idea that there was anything noble and good about our nation, questioning whether we had a Christian value system worth sharing with others.

National disenchantment, erupting from the "devaluing" of our heritage, reached its climax during the Vietnam War. Men and women who believed that we had something worth defending were fighting, dying and spilling their blood on the foreign soil of Vietnam. Meanwhile, back home, students were being told that "Our old values are not worth fighting and dying for." Tragically, America lost its heroes, its vision, and the principles upon which our nation had been anchored from its conception.

A BRIEF LOOK AT GOD'S ROLE IN OUR NATION'S HISTORY

Our nation sprung from a group of thirteen colonies, united in war, driven by a desire for liberty. Was there a God-consciousness in the conception of these colonies, or was the motivation purely materialistic? Look at these key historical facts:[2]

- The Virginia Charter of 1609 says, "The principle effect which we can expect or desire of this action is the conversion of the people in those parts unto the true worship of God and the Christian religion."

- The Pilgrim Charter of 1620 states that its purpose was "to advance the enlargement of the Christian religion to the glory of God Almighty."

- Before the pilgrims stepped off the Mayflower, they signed the Mayflower Compact, making it clear that the move to the colonies was being done "for the glory of God."

- In 1630 the Puritans came to our shores and said, "We are entered into a covenant with Him [that is with God] for this work."

- In 1632, when Maryland was chartered as a colony, they wrote, "We are motivated with a pious zeal for extending the Christian religion."

- The North Carolina charter reads: the work was begun "for the propagation of the Gospel."

- Rhode Island's charter, reads, "We are to pursue this with most holy Christian faith."

- A British governor, sent by the Board of Trade of Great Britain to the Colonies to govern the affairs of trade between the Colonies and Great Britain, responded by letter to their concern over the lack of cooperation by the colonies: "If you ask an American who is his master, he will tell you that he has none, nor any governor but Jesus Christ."

- The final sentence of the Declaration of Independence, signed July 4, 1776, states, "For the support of this declaration, with a firm reliance upon the protection of Divine Providence, we mutually pledge to each other, our lives, our fortunes, and our sacred honor."

- Eight days after the signing of the declaration, when the Liberty Bell was rung, it had printed on its side a quote from Leviticus 25:10: *"Proclaim liberty throughout all the land unto all the inhabitants thereof."*

DID NATIONAL LEADERS SEE EVIDENCE OF GOD'S PROVIDENCE?

It is interesting to note that in his journal, George Washington, whom many contemporary historians have inaccurately described as an impious and perverted man, recorded his personal conversion to the Lord Jesus Christ. Also, when asked to comment on the Revolutionary War, he said, "The hand of Providence has been so conspicuous in all this that he must be worse than an infidel and more than wicked that has no gratitude enough to acknowledge this obligation." Still later Washington noted, "I am sure that never was there a people who had more reason to acknowledge a divine interposition in their affairs than those of the United States. I should be pained to believe that they had forgotten the agency which ever so often was manifested in this Revolution."

A Critical Moment In The Life Of The Constitution

When men gathered to write a constitution for this new nation, it was not, at first, an amicable convention. There was a great deal of arguing and disputing over the petty self interests of the various states. James Madison, often called the Father and Architect of the Constitution, kept meticulous notes during the Constitutional Convention. He recorded a crucial statement which reveals the important role the founders of our nation believed God must play in our nation's formation. As tempers flared and little was being accomplished, Benjamin Franklin, eighty-one years old, stood and addressed George Washington:

"In this situation of this assembly, groping as it were in the dark, to find political truth, and scarce able to distinguish it when presented to us, how has it happened, Sir, that we have not hitherto once thought of humbly appealing to the Father of Lights to illuminate our understanding. In the beginning of the contest with Great Britain, when we were sensible of great danger, we had daily prayer in this room for Divine protection. Our prayers, Sir, were heard. And they were graciously answered. All of us who were engaged in this struggle must have observed frequent instances of a superintending Providence in our favor. To that kind of Providence, we owe this happy opportunity of consulting in peace on the means of establishing our future national felicity. And have we forgotten this powerful Friend or do we imagine that we no longer need His assistance? I have lived, Sir, a long time, and the longer I live, the more convincing proofs I see of this truth, that God governs in the affairs of men. And if a sparrow cannot fall to the ground without His notice, is it probable an empire can raise without His aid? We have been assured, sir, in the Sacred Writings that 'except the Lord build the house, they labor in vain that build it.' I firmly believe this, and I also believe that without His concurring aid, we shall succeed in our little building no better than the builders of Babel. We shall be divided by our partial local interests, our projects will be confounded. We ourselves will become a reproach and a byword in future years. And what is worse, mankind may hereafter, from this unfortunate instance, despair of establishing governments by human wisdom and leave it to chance, war, and conquest. I therefore beg leave to move that henceforth, prayers imploring the assistance of Heaven and its blessings on our deliberation, be heard in this assembly every morning before we proceed to do business, and that one or more of the local clergy of this city, be requested to officiate in this service."[3]

The motion passed, the convention moved into smooth seas, and one of the world's most unique documents was birthed under the watchful eye of God. Madison, writing later about the Constitutional Convention, noted, "We have staked the whole future of American civilization not upon the power of government - far from it. We have staked the future of our political institutions upon the capacity of mankind for self-government, upon the capacity of each and all of us to govern ourselves, to control ourselves, to sustain ourselves according to the Ten Commandments of God."[4]

Here is the point: our heritage is distinctly divine, and if our government is to work at all, it will only work among a people who acknowledge the sovereignty of God and their responsibility to Him. American history cannot be accurately seen apart from the spiritual motivations and convictions of its founders.

II. THERE IS A PERVERSION WHICH WILL DESTROY THE HOPE OF THIS NATION

God warned the Israelites to *"Beware, lest you forget the Lord who brought you out of the land of Egypt, from the house of bondage" (Deuteronomy 6:12).* In this century, every branch of the government has given evidence of "forgetting the Lord" and

His role in our nation's history. This is most obvious in the Supreme Court's "new" interpretation of the First Amendment to the Constitution.

When many people think of the First Amendment, they immediately think of "separation of church and state." In reality, it has nothing to do with separation of church and state. The words "separation of church and state" are not even in the First Amendment. The portion of the amendment which pertains to freedom of expression and religion is comprised of sixteen words which simply state: "Congress shall make no law respecting the establishment of religion or prohibiting the free exercise thereof."

The original concern, prompting the writing of the First Amendment, was a fear of government religion - a fear that America, like England, would have a "state church," which would require worship and be supported by taxes. This fear of the Church of England is highlighted in one of the earlier drafts of the amendment, the word "denomination" was used instead of the word "religion." Even the most recent commentaries on the Constitution state that the whole purpose of the amendment was to prohibit the government from establishing a state religion and that religious expression was to be protected from state intervention and government suppression. America was to be a country where people of all faiths could worship without fear of any retribution.

Where did the idea of "separation of church and state" originate? In a 1947 Supreme Court case, Everson versus The Board of Education, the court made an unparalleled decision. Referring to an obscure statement written in a letter by Thomas Jefferson, they shifted from their responsibility of interpreting the Constitution based on the founders' intentions and instead, rendered a decision which in essence, re-interpreted the Constitution. Here was their new position: "The First Amendment has erected a wall between church and state. That wall must be kept high and impregnable. We could not approve the slightest breach." From that point on, whenever the Supreme Court has ruled on a religious issue, its tendency has not been to refer to the Constitution, but rather to that 1947 statement regarding "a wall between church and state."

The most crucial application of this new policy was in the June 25, 1962 decision in the Engel versus Vitale case regarding prayer in public schools. The issue was the reciting of the following prayer in a public school: "Almighty God, we acknowledge our dependence upon Thee, and we beg Thy blessing upon us, our parents, our teachers, and our country." The reciting of that prayer in a public school was ruled unconstitutional by the Supreme Court. From that moment, America, despite its unique heritage, began to self-destruct.

What has happened to America since 1962? Has the situation improved or deteriorated? David Barton, founder of Wall Builders, Inc., in his book The Myth of Separation has chronicled the devastating "domino effect" since the original decision. Examine the following Supreme Court rulings to see the clear picture of deterioration:

- 1965 - freedom of speech is guaranteed unless the topic is religion.

- 1965 - it is unconstitutional for any student to pray over his lunch.

- 1967 - it is unconstitutional for kindergartners to recite this prayer: "We thank you for the flowers sweet, we thank you for the food we eat, we thank you for the birds that sing, we thank you for everything." (Even though the word "God" is not mentioned, the Supreme Court said someone might construe it as a prayer.)

- 1969 - it is unconstitutional for a war memorial to be erected in the shape of a cross.

- 1970 - it is unconstitutional for students to arrive at school early and hear a student volunteer read from the Congressional Record the prayers offered by the chaplains of the House and Senate. (All the proceedings of the Congress and the Senate are recorded in the Congressional Record).

- 1979 - Boards of Education may no longer use the word "God" in their writings.
- 1979 - it is unconstitutional for a class to ask in an assembly whose birthday is celebrated at Christmas.
- 1980 - it is unconstitutional for the Ten Commandments to hang on the wall of a classroom because "...students might meditate on them, respect them, and ultimately obey them."
- 1984 - a bill is unconstitutional - though its wording may be correct - if the legislator had a religious activity in his mind when he wrote it.
- 1984 - it is unconstitutional for students in a classroom to recite the prayer, "God is great, God is good, let us thank Him for our food."
- 1985 - it is unconstitutional for a graduation ceremony to include an opening or closing prayer.

Ironically, these decisions came from a Supreme Court which opens its sessions with the words, "God save the United States and this honorable court." As they sat to render these decisions, (which struck down the role of God, prayer, religion and Scriptural principles), they were under the ominous, piercing gaze of Moses, carved in relief on the wall of their chamber, holding the Ten Commandments.[5] We've come a long way from the Supreme Court ruling of 1840 which stated, "The purest principles of morality are to be taught in our schools. Where are they found? Whoever searches for them must go to the source from which a Christian man derives his faith - that is his Bible."[6]

I am indebted once again to David Barton, this time for his book America, To Pray or Not to Pray?[7] When asked the question, "Do you think there have been many consequences since the Supreme Court ruling in 1962?" - he began a study which led to startling conclusions. Since 1962:

- Average SAT scores have dropped by over 80 points.

- Abortions (on the decrease prior to 1962) now average 1.7 million annually.

- Violent crime (also in decline prior to 1962) has now increased to unprecedented levels.

- More than 50% of marriages end in divorce (which was the exception rather than the rule prior to 1962).

- We have gone from being the greatest creditor nation in the world to being the greatest debtor nation in the world.

- Private enterprise has declined 70% since 1962.

- One million high school students drop out of school each year. Prior to 1962 most students who started high school also completed it.

- In 1962, only 4% of high school students had tried drugs, as compared to 80% in 1990.

While you must read Barton's study to gain a complete perspective, here is an important point: prior to 1962, in areas of morality, education, human ethic and productivity, the American society was moving forward. In the thirty years since that Supreme Court ruling, there has been an unraveling of our society. While we can't place the complete blame on the issue of prayer in schools, this ominous fact remains: **the Supreme Court decision regarding prayer in public schools was perhaps the first outright defiant statement against God that the highest court of our land had ever made.**

It is ironic that, on the one hand we print on our coins "In God We Trust," and in our pledge we say we are "One nation under God," and the Senate and House begin with prayer every morning; yet on the other hand, our nation's highest court is trying to eliminate every vestige of God from our institutions. How can we escape the judgment of God Who said, *"The Lord your God is a jealous God among you, lest the anger of the Lord be aroused against you and destroy you from the face of the earth"* (Deuteronomy 6:15).

It has been said that our generation could be the first generation in the history of America which would not hand to the next generation a better life and nation than the one they themselves received. This is a tragedy which must be avoided. But is there a plan by which we can salvage the heart of America? Will America experience revival? There will be no reformation in our land until first there is a revival of the Christian faith in our land. We must once again move under God's protection.

III. THERE IS A PATHWAY WHICH CAN DELIVER THE HEART OF OUR NATION

While the second half of this book presents "revival" as the ultimate answer to our nation's problems, there are some specific steps every devoted believer in Christ will want to take regarding the free expression of religion.

1) It is time to energetically embrace the constitutionally guaranteed privileges which are yours. Do not be intimidated by people who keep using the issue of "separation of church and state." Understand what is legally available to you and know your constitutional rights. For instance, revival can take root in the hearts of our nation's youth. Students, here are your rights:[8]

- You have the right to meet with other students on your campus for religious purposes. That is guaranteed by the Equal Access Right.
- You have the right to identify your religious beliefs with signs and with symbols.
- You have the right to talk about your religious beliefs on your campus.
- You have the right to distribute Christian literature.
- You have the right to pray on campus. (The Supreme Court ruling had to do with state-mandated prayer.)

- You have the right to carry and study your Bible on campus. (The Supreme Court only addressed state-directed Bible studies.)

- You have the right to do your research papers, speeches, and creative projects on religious themes.

- You have the right to be exempt from classes if a teacher is teaching something that contradicts your religious beliefs.

- You have the right to celebrate or study religious holidays on campus as long as it is presented as a traditional part of the American culture studied in an objective sense.

- You have the right to meet with school officials.

Exercise the rights that you do have. America is still the best place in the world to live.

2) Be sure you know the positions of your elected and appointed officials on critical issues and vote your conscience. Don't always vote with your party if you question their stand on a certain issue. If you are not registered to vote and you are of voting age, you have no right to complain about the government. No vote, no gripe.

3) Never assign to the government a responsibility God has specifically assigned to you; they cannot produce the same positive results. The school is not intended to make up for a Godless home. The education system is not designed as a substitute for parental involvement in the lives of children. Remember, you *"shall teach them diligently to your children, and shalt talk of them when you sit in your house, and when you walk by the way, and when you lie down and when you rise up. And you shall bind them for a sign on your hand, and they shall be as frontlets between your eyes"* (Deuteronomy 6:7-8). That is a parent's responsibility.

4) If your child attends school outside the home, you have a right to get involved in your child's education. After all, you are paying for it and you are providing the student. A good educator realizes that a school, at its absolute best, is nothing more than an extension of what should be learned in the home.

5) Remember that you teach by example. There's no use in getting distressed about the Supreme Court's ruling on prayer if you don't pray anyway. The greatest thing any parent has to share with a child is a Godly value system and a personal faith in Christ.

A FINAL OBSERVATION

At the heart of education is the whole matter of discipline. It is estimated that discipline may comprise as much as 60-70% of the whole education process. Where there is no respect for authority, there is no learning.

With God far removed from the classroom, discipline has become a matter of force, intellect and logic. Classrooms have become chaotic. The America system is not designed to operate on respect created by intimidation. It is based upon the fact that people who acknowledge a sovereign God will respect others and submit to His divinely appointed authority. This is why the Supreme Court's decision, which in effect diminished the role of God in the classroom, precipitated attitudes and events causing America to begin to self destruct.

Revival

Gypsy Smith was once asked how to start a revival. He answered: "Go home, lock yourself in your room, and kneel down in the middle of your floor. Draw a chalk mark all around yourself and ask God to start the revival inside that chalk mark. When He has answered your prayer, the revival will be on."

Missionary Worker

5

Setting the Stage
For Revival

"If My people who are called by My name will humble themselves, and pray and seek My face, and turn from their wicked ways, then I will hear from Heaven, and will forgive their sin and heal their land. Now My eyes will be open and My ears attentive to prayer made in this place" (2 Chronicles 7:14-15).

The first four chapters of this book give rise to the question: Is it too late to turn back? It is obvious that we are in desperate need of national reform. Without it, America, which is now on the edge, will soon lose its place of influence among the nations of the world and having sown seeds of destruction, we will begin to reap the fruit of God's wrath. Is there any hope for our nation or any nation so desperately in need of reformation?

History records that positive reformation is always preceded by national revival. And more specifically, national revival is preceded by a revival in God's church and among individuals who are called by His name. In the balance of this book, we will examine the great revival text of 2 Chronicles 7:14. Before we study this promise phrase by phrase, there are three general observations worthy of our attention, which will help set the stage for revival.

I. GOD IS WILLING TO BRING REVIVAL

The fact that God revealed to Solomon a plan for revival indicates His willingness to move among His people and restore fellowship with them. There are conditions which must be met, but when they are, the Lord says *"then will I hear from Heaven and will forgive their sin and will heal their land."*

The purpose in praying for revival is not that we might overcome God's reluctance to bring revival but that our reluctant and recalcitrant hearts might be brought into concert with God's heart and His will for our lives. We do not pray in order to get God's attention because as His children, we already have His undivided attention. Instead, our prayers expose the barrenness of our hearts which prompts us to seek God for a mighty work of His grace.

Some people pray as if they are attempting to get God's sympathy for a life gone astray, but God will never sympathize with sin. I was once asked by a broken-hearted mother if I would pray with her for her son. As we knelt to pray, she began, "Now Lord, you know my son is a good boy." Hearing that statement, I tapped her on the shoulder and said, "I don't believe we're here to impress God with your son's goodness. We're kneeling here in prayer because your son is far away from God." While God is not willing to "bend" His will or standards to accommodate our half-hearted appeals, He is willing to bring forgiveness, cleansing and restored fellowship if we will bring our broken lives before Him in prayer. In fact, He has assured us that *"a broken and a contrite heart He will not despise"* (Psalm 51:17). God is willing to bring revival.

II. GOD IS WAITING TO BRING REVIVAL

"Now My eyes will be open and My ears attentive to prayer made in this place" (2 Chronicles 7:15).   God is watching and listening for our response to His call for revival.

Years ago, a young man wrote home to his parents asking for severely needed funds to complete his college education. He was dismayed when his parents only sent him a new Bible in response to his request. In its fly-leaf they had written these words: "The answer to all of your life's needs is found in this book. Philippians 4:19"   The young man was so aggravated with his parents response, he wrote them a harsh letter expressing his anger and disappointment. He received a loving response from his parents, simply encouraging him to be a man of God's Word and to faithfully study the Bible. But there was no money enclosed in that letter either.   One day, after weeks of agonizing silence and mounting financial pressure, in desperation, the young man took the Bible in hand and with bitter tears confessed the hardness of his heart before God. He turned to Philippians 4:19 and read, *"My God shall supply all your need according to His riches in glory by Christ Jesus."* Carefully tucked in that page was an amount of money far surpassing his original request. His parents had simply been waiting for him to comply with their encouragement that he be a man of God's Word.

In a similar fashion, God is waiting to bring revival to us. Tucked away among the phrases, *"If My people, who are called by My name, will humble themselves and pray and seek My face, and turn from their wicked ways..."*   are the great promises and resources for revival. God is simply waiting for us to heed His request.

III. SOMETHING IS WANTING ON OUR PART

If God is *willing* to bring revival and if God is *waiting* to bring revival, then why doesn't revival come? The answer is simple: Something is *wanting* on our part. The prerequisites for revival, that which is wanting, is clearly spelled out, *"If My people, who are called by My name, will **humble themselves**, and **pray and seek My face**, and **turn from their wicked ways;** then I will hear from Heaven, and will forgive their sin and heal their land."* Revival is ultimately a sovereign work of a holy God, and yet, God in His sovereignty tells us that He is predisposed to bring revival to those people who exhibit the earnest desire for revival by seeking to meet the clearly stated prerequisites.

On the following pages, we will examine in detail each of these six prerequisites. I firmly believe that it is our responsibility to at least set the stage for revival, to do all we can do from a human stand point. Then we must simply trust God to do what only He can do - bring the refreshing and restoration so desperately needed.

Is it too late to turn back? Hopefully, for our nation and for our individual lives, the answer is "No!" Certainly, genuine national, moral and political reformation must be preceded by genuine spiritual revival. But history clearly reminds us that God is under no obligation to bring revival to people who consistently reject Him. While it may not be too late today, tomorrow it could be. My prayer is that at the end of every chapter, you will prayerfully consider your responsibility to God and that God will hear from our hearts, both individually and as a nation, a great concert of earnest prayer for Heaven-sent revival. Now, let's set the stage for revival.

6

The Three Certain Signs of Salvation

"If My People..."

"For as many as are led by the Spirit of God, these are sons of God. For you did not receive the spirit of bondage again to fear, but you received the Spirit of adoption by whom we cry out "Abba, Father." The Spirit Himself bears witness with our spirit that we are children of God..." (Romans 8:14-16).

Several years ago my family went on vacation with another family. We went up to the great Northwest and enjoyed a time of recreation, fellowship, and inspiration from God. One afternoon we decided to have some friendly, family competition, so I said, "I want all the Elliff family to come over here." Immediately, my children and my wife made a circle around me on the court. I didn't see my children casting about saying, "Am I an Elliff?" There was an immediate recognition in their heart of who they were. They were part of the Elliff family.

If the Lord Jesus came to earth again and said, "All the people who are part of God's family come and stand by Me," would you have to sit and think for a moment whether you are part of God's family? Or, would you immediately know that He was speaking of you?

It is the singular nature of revival that it can only happen to God's people. Others will always benefit from the effects of revival, but revival itself is a sovereign work of God among His people.

Not everyone is part of God's family. I know there is an idealistic dream taught in the New Age movement that the entire world is part of God's family, but the Bible says there is a unique group of people on this earth who are, in fact, born again into the family of God. Yes, there is a sense in which all mankind is similar; we share some things together, and we're all His creation, but we're **not** all members of His family. The great revival passage in 2 Chronicles 7:14 opens by targeting a specific audience: *"If My people..."*.

Any individual, church, or nation seeking revival must first follow the admonition of the Apostle Paul to *"Examine yourselves as to whether you are in the faith. Prove yourselves"* (2 Corinthians 13:5). Contrary to popular belief, an intense personal examination of your relationship to Christ is both a Scriptural and necessary prerequisite for revival. Many churches fall into prolonged periods of spiritual deadness because they do not heed Paul's command to the church at Corinth that each member should examine himself.

Over the years, I have counseled many faithful church members who, despite all of their dedicated activity, were keenly aware that something was desperately wrong in their relationship with God. Many of them have confessed to years of doubt about the genuineness of their salvation. Others indicate that they have slipped into the meaningless and futile habit of daily asking the Lord to save them "just in case they are not already saved." That prayer does nothing but add confusion to an already troubled heart because it is not born out of a deep conviction of sin nor does it bring the sweet certainty of salvation.

In 1 Corinthians 11:28, Paul once again tells the Corinthian church to, *"let a man examine himself."* He is referring to the kind of proof that comes from testing. So at the beginning of the journey to revival, it is both expedient and profitable to <u>examine</u>

yourself, to see if you are really targeted in the statement *"if My people."* But what questions should you ask? And what evidences should you seek? The following will serve as a simple guide:

I. Am I On An Upward Path?

Paul indicates that those who are the sons of God are those who are *"led by the Spirit of God"* (Romans 8:14). It is worth considering whether, from the moment you have identified as the point of your conversion, you have been consciously aware of God's leading in your life and have been on an upward spiritual path. This does never mean that the pilgrimage of your life will never be marked by lapses, stumbling, moments of great failure and disappointment, or battles with besetting sin. You might think of your life's journey as being similar to that of a mountain climber whose path consists of many "ups and downs." Although his general direction is upward, at times he must go downward in order to find a clearer path. From a distance, however, we would observe that, regardless of his struggles and brief descents, the overall direction of his path is upward.

There is a common perception today that "becoming" a Christian can be separated from "being" a Christian. But they are inseparable. Often, a person thinks he is saved because he can remember that he "prayed the prayer." But what about his life since then? Has he grown closer to the Lord or farther apart? Has there been little or no spiritual growth in his life since the point of his conversion? Would having heard him pray twenty years ago be the same as hearing him pray today? Is his devotional life different? Are his commitments different? Has his sensitivity to sin and hatred of it diminished or grown? Change is an evidence of conversion.

The thought that "becoming" a Christian can be separated from "being" a Christian is errant and must be replaced by the correct and Scriptural perspective. The Scripture clearly teaches that we are not saved by our good works (Ephesians 2:8-9), but the Scripture also clearly states that people who are genuinely born again will give evidence of their salvation by their behavior. In other words, belief cannot be separated from behavior.

In the Sermon on the Mount, our Lord reminded us that *"not everyone who says to Me, Lord, Lord, shall enter the kingdom of Heaven, but he who does the will of my Father in Heaven"* (Matthew 7:21). On another occasion, He chided those who called Him Lord and yet did not do what He said (Luke 6:46). The point is, true saving faith affects the way we behave.

One of the most sobering statements in Scripture regarding the change that takes place in the life of a believer is found in 1 John 3:6-9.

> *Whoever abides in Him does not sin. Whoever sins has neither seen Him nor known Him. Little children, let no one deceive you. He who practices righteousness is righteous, just as He is righteous. He who sins is of the devil, for the devil has sinned from the beginning. For this purpose the Son of God was manifested, that He might destroy the works of the devil. Whoever has been born of God does not sin, for His seed remains in him; and he cannot sin, because he has been born of God.*

In this passage the references to sin imply a "continual sense." For instance, we might read the passage this way, "Whosoever abides in Him does not keep on committing the same old sins in the same old way."

For too long people have excused their spiritual deadness by including themselves in that group they call "the backslidden." But earlier in John's letter, he points out that anyone who is habitually "backslidden" has probably never been genuinely born into God's family. *"They went out from us, but they were not of us; for if they had been of us, they would have continued with us: but they went out, that they might be made manifest, that none of them were of us"* (1 John 2:19).

The fact that genuine salvation produces Godly behavior is irrefutably stated in Hebrews 11 - the roll-call of the great men and women of faith. As you read this passage, you will discover that not one of these individuals is famous simply because of what he or she thought or felt. Each one is famous for the <u>behavior</u> which characterized his or her faith; Able <u>offered</u>, Enoch <u>walked</u>, Noah <u>prepared</u>, Abraham <u>went out</u>. In other words, though we are not saved by works, neither are we saved by the kind of faith which does not produce good works.

Some years ago, I heard the chaplain of a Rotary club pray this prayer: "Lord, be with these Rotarians today, for we know Thy way is the Rotary way." This misguided man had reduced his expectations of the remarkable change which takes place at conversion to the point that it was no more demanding than the creed of a community service group. With all due respects to this good organization, meeting Jesus, passing from death to life, having old things pass away and all things become new, having your destination changed from an eternity in hell to an eternity in Heaven, surrendering your life to the One who is the Creator and the Sustainer of the universe, and acknowledging Him as King of kings and Lord of lords will produce a life which is so different no mere creed can embody it. For this reason, the first certain sign of salvation is a life on an upward path.

II. Have I Made An Outward Profession?

"For you did not receive the spirit of bondage again to fear, but you received the Spirit of adoption, by whom we cry out 'Abba, Father'" (Romans 8:15). "Abba" is a word of tender endearment and communion. It is more like the word "daddy" than the more formal word "father." Paul is saying that the true believer, set free from the bondage of sin and the law and adopted as a child of God, is not intimidated as he openly cries out to the Father on the basis of a new and intimate relationship.

In the passage above there is a sense of eagerness to confess the Lord. Jesus even indicated that the fear of "confession" before men indicates a lack of "possession" of genuine salvation. *"Therefore whoever confesses Me before men, him I will also confess before My Father who is in Heaven. But whoever denies Me before men, him I will also deny before My Father who is in Heaven"* (Matthew 10:32-33).

Many people think that anything which is personal should also be kept private. When asked about their salvation, they will tell you that their religion is a personal matter. While it is a personal matter, it was never intended to be kept private or secret. My marriage ceremony was an intensely personal issue, but it was not private, and the ring I wear on my finger is a constant visual reminder to everyone I meet that I belong to someone.

The Lord is so interested in our outward profession that He even included it as a part of His great commission. Disciples were not only to be "made" but were also to be "marked" by the ordinance of baptism, which is a picture that one has died to an old way of life and risen to newness of life. This new life is to be characterized by the new behavior expected of the first disciples. *"Teaching them to observe (or do) all things that I have commanded you"* (Matthew 28:20). Every believer should be unashamed to say it, show it, and share it. Jesus indicated that those who love Him will keep His commandments, and those who subscribe to His Lordship will do what He says.

Many professing believers have no sense of victory in their lives because they stubbornly refuse to follow the Lord's commands regarding an outward profession of faith. I remember one prominent church leader confessing that after having been baptized as a young man, he later became deeply convicted of his sin and his need of genuine salvation. In deep brokenness he received Christ by faith. The next Sunday, when the altar call was given in his church, he started to go down the aisle and tell his pastor what had happened, but then he thought, "I'm a church leader. People would be disillusioned if they thought I had been in a position of leadership all these years and was not genuinely saved. Making this decision would cause confusion, and I certainly don't want to do that. Anyway, salvation is a personal matter, and what really matters is that I have trusted Christ."

With tears this man confessed to me that through the years he was far more concerned about what men thought of him than what God thought of him. He then admitted that he knew there would never be spiritual victory in his life until he made an outward profession of his faith. When he did openly confess his faith before his church family, many other men, in brokenness and with tears, came to the altar to receive Christ and follow Him in Scriptural baptism.

It is for precisely this reason that our Lord demands an outward profession on the part of those who know Him.

III. Do I Have An Inward Peace?

Romans 8:16 should encourage every believer *"The Spirit Himself bears witness with our spirit that we are children of God..."* Here is the crucial, final and inescapable evidence of genuine salvation. It is the witness of God's Holy Spirit with our spirit, affirming to us that we belong to God.

When people ask me to help them discover whether they are truly born again, I often encourage them to pray, asking God to speak to them through 1 John because John's first letter sheds great light on the evidences of salvation. In 1 John 4:13 we are reminded that, *"By this we know that we abide in Him, and He in us, because He has given us of His Spirit."*

I have known people who were in such turmoil about their salvation that they would play intellectual gymnastics with the issue. "Let's see," they would say, "in Revelation 3:20 Jesus said He would come into my heart if I asked Him. I have asked Him, therefore, He must be in my heart." Unfortunately, mind games never really help, because peace never comes, and the doubts return: "Am I really saved? Did I say the right words? Have I done the right things? Was I really sincere? Did I have enough faith?" And since every preacher they hear has a different way of describing the conversion experience, they find themselves on a spiritual merry-go-round growing dizzy with all the suggestions of different prayers, postures and performances.

Here is what Paul is telling us: After you strip away your "conversion experience," your good life, your church membership, and even the testimony of others who tell you "If <u>anybody</u> is saved, <u>you're</u> saved," the truly born again person still has a deep underlying sense of assurance that is given him by the Spirit of God. None of the former will get you into Heaven, and in fact, there are many people who have all of those spiritual dominoes properly aligned and yet doubt remains. What is missing is the witness of God's Spirit.

While in college and dating my wife to be, I was perplexed to hear her say on more than one occasion, "Sometimes I wonder if I am really saved." I just knew she must be a Christian. After all, she had made her decision in one of the largest churches in that state and was baptized by one of the most noted pastors in the area. She had grown up in the church and even surrendered her life to the "call to missions." Our first date was to a Wednesday night worship service when she was leading a missions group for young girls! Everything about her life indicated she was a Christian.

During the early years of our marriage, when Jeannie again expressed doubts about her salvation, I logically convinced her that she was truly born again. But God's Spirit prevailed! In the fourth year of our marriage, she told me, "It makes no difference what either of us say or think, **I don't have inward peace!** I know I am lost!" That night she became a new creature in Christ.

It would be difficult for me to describe the change that occurred in her life. I thought she was already a perfect lady, but her transformed life became a challenge to me. Her insatiable hunger for the Word of God was one of the most notable changes. Also, she developed an earnest desire to see others come to Christ. Within hours of her conversion, she stood before the church, confessed her faith, and followed the Lord in baptism. Through the years, she has repeatedly remarked about the wonderful peace which the Spirit of God brought to her heart.

Many people go through life with re-curring doubts about the issue of their salvation. They often pray what I call the "Nothing

Prayer." "Lord, if I'm not save, save me." It is a "nothing prayer" because it is not born out of a genuine conviction that they are lost. Nor does it bring certainty of salvation. If it did, they would have no need to repeat it again and again. The Spirit would bear witness with their spirit that they were a child of God.

Some years ago, after preaching this message on the evidences of salvation, I was confronted by an irritated church member who exclaimed, "You're just trying to sow doubt in the hearts of these fine church members. We are all right with God, and we don't need to ask any questions about our faith!" Beneath the anger, I sensed a tinge of fear, a fear that an examination of himself would prove that true faith was missing. But sadly, he would not examine himself. Had he done so and found himself outside the faith, it would have been a simple matter to repent of sin and unbelief and turn to Christ for genuine salvation. And if in the process of examination he found himself to be a member of God's family, then he would have been a candidate for genuine revival. Genuine revival comes to those of whom the Lord says "These are My people."

7

How Are
You Known?

"...which are called by My name..."

"Then, six days before the Passover, Jesus came to Bethany, where Lazarus was who had been dead, whom He had raised from the dead. There they made Him a supper; and Martha served, but Lazarus was one of those who sat at the table with Him. Then Mary took a pound of very costly oil of spikenard, anointed the feet of Jesus, and wiped His feet with her hair. And the house was filled with the fragrance of the oil. Then one of His disciples, Judas Iscariot, Simon's son, who would betray Him, said, 'Why was this fragrant oil not sold for three hundred denarii and given to the poor?' This he said, not that he cared for the poor, but because he was a thief, and had the money box; and he used to take what was put in it. But Jesus said, 'Let her alone; she has kept this for the day of My burial. For the poor you have with you always, but Me you do not have always.' Then a great many of the Jews knew that He was there; and they came, not for Jesus' sake only, but that they might also see Lazarus, whom He had raised from the dead. But the chief priests took counsel that they might also put Lazarus to death, because on account of him many of the Jews went away and believed in Jesus" (John 12:1-11).

The mere mention of one's name often causes others to immediately recall specific characteristics associated with that person. The name Benedict Arnold, for instance, is associated with his betrayal of American confidence during the Revolutionary War. Vicious cruelty and anti-semitism are associated with the name Adolf Hitler. The qualities of thoughtfulness and principle are associated with Abraham Lincoln. We speak of the faith of Abraham, the courage of Daniel, and the wisdom of Solomon. On the other hand, there is doubting Thomas and Judas, the betrayer.

What qualities come to mind at the mention of your name? When your name is spoken, do people make note of the fact (if not verbally, at least mentally) that you are a believer in Christ? Is your relationship with Jesus the first thing that people think of when they think about you? How are you known? The Lord said that a prerequisite for revival is not just that we <u>are</u> His, but that we are <u>called</u> His.

In John 12, we meet three people who are called by His name: Lazarus and his sisters, Mary and Martha. Their lives exhibit at least four characteristics which will be evident in those who are called by the name of the Lord.

I. YOU WILL HAVE BEEN TOUCHED BY THE LORD IN A MIGHTY WAY

It is interesting to note that when people thought about Lazarus, it was Lazarus, "the one who had been raised from the dead." Granted, that is a particularly dramatic description, but you do not have to have been raised from physical death in order for people to know that you are an individual with whom God has dealt in a mighty way. Let me suggest three areas in which others should notice God's mighty dealings in your life.

First, He should have **dealt with you in deliverance** - deliverance *from* sin with all of its bondage and slavery, and *into* His wonderful life. Your acquaintances ought to know that you have been genuinely born again into the family of God. If they have known you for any length of time, they should have heard you declare that Jesus has rescued you from sin and an eternity in Hell. Your life should be consistent with the testimony of your lips. Just as God delivered Lazarus from physical death, people should recognized that God has delivered you from spiritual death.

Second, people should know that **God has poured out great blessings on your life.** They recognized that Lazarus was a blessed individual. Are your acquaintances aware of how God has blessed you? So often, our friends know about our prayer requests, they have heard about our needs and our problems, but we forget to tell them how God has moved in might and power to pour out His blessing on our lives. When your name is mentioned in conversation, do people immediately recall God's blessing on your life?

Third, you should be known as someone in whose life **God has exercised discipline.** One of the great evidences of the second birth is that God treats you like one of His children, not only in blessing, but in discipline. As a matter of fact, your willingness to share how God has disciplined you when you have been found moving away from His will for your life will bring a sense of reality and transparency to your testimony. People will be encouraged to know that He has been faithful to "hem you up" to His will.

Some years ago, I read the testimony of C. L. Cullpepper, a missionary to China. From that moment, I had an intense desire to meet this great man of God. His life and ministry were associated with the marvelous moving of God's Spirit in China during the Shantung revival. He, along with the other missionaries in that province, witnessed the remarkable turning to Christ of thousands of Chinese. Years later, I had the privilege of meeting Dr. Cullpepper. In his 80's, he stood before our congregation and spoke like a great patriarch of God. God used him like a fire-brand to touch the hearts of everyone present that evening.

In the closing moments of his message, Dr. Cullpepper, with a moving moment of transparency, related a specific incident which showed how God had dealt with him and his family in a mighty way. He told of the distress in his heart when, upon his arrival in China, he watched how the Chinese, hoping to appease the dog gods, would place their deceased children in shallow graves where they could be easily recovered by the wild dogs in the community. On the very first day of his new mission assignment, he saw a dog dragging a portion of a child's body down the street. His heart was broken because of this heathen practice. Later in his room and on his knees, he prayed, "Dear God in Heaven, if there is some way that I can show these people what death means for a Christian, then I would be willing."

In less than a year, the Cullpepper's small child was stricken with a dreaded disease and soon died. C. L. Cullpepper walked out behind the mission compound and challenged God to show him why his precious treasure had been taken away. Suddenly, he remembered the first prayer he prayed upon his arrival in China. It dawned on him that the death of his child could be used of God to speak to the heart of the Chinese in that community. A Christian funeral was planned, the very first the Chinese had ever witnessed. People came from all around and heard, for the first time and with willing hearts, the wonderful gospel of the Lord Jesus. It was obvious to them that God had dealt with the Cullpepper family in a mighty way. From that moment on, the work in that province was established and powerfully blessed.

Are you willing for God to deal with your life in such a powerful fashion that others will associate His grace, His love, and His power with you and your experience? To be "called by His name" means that others see you as a person whose life has been touched by God in a mighty fashion.

II. YOU WILL POSSESS A GREAT REVERENCE FOR GOD

In this Scripture passage, Martha served the supper and Lazarus sat at the table with Jesus, but it was Mary who took a pound of very costly spices and anointed His feet. This was an act of extravagant love born out of deep reverence. As she wiped His feet with her hair, the house was filled with the fragrance of the perfume. Later, Mary would be fondly remembered for this act of reverence (see John 11:2). This was not the first time Mary worshiped the Lord while others were busy and distracted. In Luke 10, we are told that Mary sat at Jesus' feet while Martha was *"distracted with all her preparations."*

Fellowship with Jesus is important, and serving Jesus is essential. But according to the Scripture, worship is primary. In Luke 10 when Martha complained that she had to do all the serving herself while Mary just sat at His feet, Jesus said, *"Martha, Martha, you are worried and troubled about many things. But one thing is needed, and Mary has chosen that good part, which will not be taken away from her."*

Worship is more than just sitting in a pew and listening to the preaching and singing. It is a matter of bringing yourself before a holy God and giving yourself in absolute surrender, adoration, and praise. When people think about you, do they sense that you have an awesome reverence and respect for Him? I am always amazed at the people who:

- say they have worshipped God but often use the Lord's name as a curse word,
- sing "all to Jesus I surrender" but only tip God when the offering plate is passed,
- claim that their body is the temple of the Holy Spirit and then assail that body with a godless habit,
- call Jesus Lord but will not obey Him.

Just how are you known? If you are truly called by His name, your life should be marked by a reverent, holy respect for Him.

In His early years, John Newton was perhaps one of the most irreverent and disrespectful people who ever walked the earth. As a teenage runaway and later a slave trader, he had such a careless disregard for human life that on more than one occasion, he literally dumped his human cargo overboard rather than be caught with illegal slaves. Once, in a drunken stupor, he fell overboard and his equally drunken friends had to rescue him by throwing a harpoon in his leg and dragging him on board. He bore the scar of that experience till the day he died.

But when John Newton came to know the Lord, his life was enveloped with a reverence for the One who had given him eternal life.

It was Newton who wrote,

> "Amazing grace, how sweet the sound that saved a wretch like me. I once was lost, but now I'm found, was blind but now I see."

While Newton lay on his deathbed, the people in the community had such great respect for him, that they placed straw on the cobblestone streets outside his window lest the rattling of passing wagons should disturb him. They had great respect for Newton, because Newton, now their pastor, had a great respect for God.

III. YOU WILL BE SENSITIVE TO WHAT THE LORD IS DOING - NOW!

People who are truly called by His name will be able to sense when God is at work. At the sight of Mary's extravagance, Judas Iscariot protested, stating that the ointment could have been sold and the money given to the poor. He sounded spiritual and charitable, as if he wanted to honor Jesus by that act of mercy. But the Scripture records that Judas, in reality, cared little for the poor and much for the money. The point is, the spiritual significance of Mary's anointing of the Lord totally escaped him. He never realized what was happening.

But people who are called by His name are just the opposite of Judas; their hearts are tuned to the Lord. They move at the prompting of the Holy Spirit and are grieved at the callous insensitivity of others. They have learned to recognize the voice of God and to identify with His heart. When they see God moving, they will go to great trouble to be part of what He is doing.

When I think of spiritually sensitive people, I often think of Fanny J. Crosby, the blind hymn writer. Someone once asked her, "Fanny, aren't you upset at what that doctor did to you? When you were just a little girl, eight years of age, he put that burning plaster on your eyes, causing you to lose your eyesight. Aren't you bitter toward that man?" But Fanny Crosby, who wrote over three thousand hymns, would reply, "Upset at the doctor? Oh no! In fact, if I could find him, I'd take him by the hand and say to him, 'Doctor, you did me the greatest favor anybody could have ever done. God used you mightily. You see, because I cannot see with my physical eyes, I have had to learn to see with my spiritual eyes. It's what I've seen with my spiritual eyes that God has used as the source for these hymns. Why, I'll have plenty of time in Heaven to look at Jesus.'" Fanny Crosby was sensitive to the moving of God.

IV. YOU WILL BE A PERSON WHOSE LIFE WILL TURN OTHERS TO CHRIST

Does your life create in other people a hunger and thirst for Jesus? A person who is filled with the Spirit will exhibit the fruit of the Spirit - love, joy, peace, long-suffering, kindness, meekness, goodness, faith, and self-control. That fruit is a picture of the character of Christ. Note that it is a cluster, which means that if you have any one of those characteristics as an evidence of the fullness of the Spirit, you will have all of them. You will not have love without joy, or peace without long-suffering.

Suppose I plant an apple tree, and over the years the tree grows and produces an abundant harvest of apples. Overjoyed at the abundance of fruit, it's only right that I decide to share it with my friends. You see, the fruit is not on the tree for the sake of the tree but for the sake of hungry people.

Unfortunately, to use the analogy above, many people assume that the fruit of the Spirit is primarily for their own enjoyment or for the enjoyment of their small circle of friends. That would be like a tree eating its own fruit!

The great purpose of revival is not for you to simply feel good, but rather that your life, through abiding in Christ, will produce such an abundance of the fruit of the Spirit, that hungry people will taste and see that the Lord is good. Your life will incite within them a desire to have what you have - Christ as Savior and Lord.

Every Tuesday morning I have the privilege of praying with a group of friends. We meet in an "upper room" at a local bank. One morning I saw a man whom I had never met before. When we gathered in small groups, I took a few moments to introduce myself to him and ask a few questions about his family and business. Then I asked if he would like to begin our prayer time. His response was interesting, "Pray? I really don't know how to pray. I'm only here because I know those men (he pointed at three men in the room) and I want what they have." He had come to the meeting because he had seen God in their lives and he wanted what he saw. Fifteen minutes later, he opened his heart to Christ and was born again. God's Holy Spirit had used the lives of his acquaintances to make him hungry for the Savior.

I have a friend who cannot pray without weeping. When he was a young man, his father taught him how to drink liquor and how to steal. On some occasions, his father would take him to a house, put him through an open window and send him around to open the front door so they could steal what was in the house. By the time he was a teenager he was an alcoholic. He would awaken some mornings having been tied to a tree by his family members in an attempt to keep him from beating on his mother and father. Later, he was discharged from the military because of his alcoholism. He was an angry and insecure man.

One day his wife convinced him to attend a worship service. That morning the preacher, moved by God's Spirit, walked right up to the man at invitation time and said, "You need to receive Jesus as your Savior." Embarrassed and humiliated, he refused

Christ then, but could not get away from the conviction of God's Spirit. A few hours later, he trusted Jesus as his Savior. God brought about a mighty change in his life. He lost his vulgar vocabulary and his desire for alcohol. Later, while he was pounding nails as part of a framing crew, God said to him, "If you can frame a house, you can also build them." He became a home builder. Then one day God said, "If you can build these things, you can sell them." So he entered the real estate business. It would be impossible for me to tell you just how many people God has touched through the life of this man who has less than a sixth grade education. But, he is known as a person whose life God has touched in a mighty way, a man who has a deep reverence for God, a man who responds to the slightest whisper of God, and a man whose life causes others to want to know his Savior.

How are you known? What is your reputation? Genuine revival is for those who are the Lord's and who are called by His name.

8

Revival's
First Step

"...shall humble themselves..."

"He who covers his sins will not prosper, but whoever confesses and forsakes them will have mercy" (Proverbs 28:13).

Permit me to introduce three people. They are fictional in nature, but I believe many people will be able to identify with the common thread running through their lives.

First, meet a pastor who is struggling in his relationship with the church to which God has called him. From the pulpit, he is calling the church to holiness. In his sermons, he often laments about the lack of "fruit" in the lives of his church members: fruit which would give evidence that Christ is in control of their lives. He is discouraged because there is little response to his preaching and virtually no response at invitation time. Deep down in his heart, he is convinced that there must be a better place for him to minister. In reality, he has grown weary of the people to whom he ministers. On occasion, he has confessed to his wife that he can't bear the thought of spending the rest of his life in that position.

He knows that he is no longer giving his best to the Lord's work. His motivation for visitation is more often guilt than eagerness to share the gospel. And when he stands to preach, he looks out across the congregation and sees more people he has disappointed than ones he has delighted. He refuses to admit it, but he now spends more time watching television than preparing his heart for ministry. His devotional life is non-existent, and he spends an inordinate amount of time on meaningless chores.

Our next person is a young seminary student who scarcely has enough time to do all he needs to do. He is busy trying to earn a living for his family, and he carries a heavy course load. Most days he is tired and frustrated. His seminary work is becoming less than meaningful. When he began seminary, his goal was to learn how to study the Word of God and impart its deep truths to others. But now he just wants to get out of school. Then, he plans to become "spiritual." He has even begun to "fudge" on his assignments, giving the impression that he is doing more work than he really is. The joy has gone from his life.

And finally, let's look at a husband who is approaching mid-life. Down deep in his heart there is a well-kept secret that he has never shared with his wife. He decided long ago that what she didn't know wouldn't hurt her. And what she doesn't know is that prior to their marriage, he was sensually and sinfully involved with another women. Sometimes, he feels that he ought to confess, but he always rationalizes his silence by thinking, "It would destroy my wife to know these facts; I love her too much to break her heart."

But lately, his wife has been cool to him. She says on occasion, "I don't feel I really know you. I feel there are hidden areas of your life through which you will not allow me to walk. Something is desperately wrong with our marriage." He's troubled by her statements, but he just can't bring himself to confess the truth.

Each of the three people you have met is experiencing the reality of Proverbs 28:13: covered sin resulting in a lack of prosperity. For God's people, the first step of revival is the step of humility. Combining both the Old and New Testament meanings of the words translated "to humble," we discover that it means literally "to bow one's knee in the heart." It means that we recognize and confess God as who He is and ourselves as who we are. In the text, we see both the costly cover-up and the clear correction for this problem.

I. THE COSTLY COVER-UP
"He who covers his sins will not prosper."

In this statement we are given a course of action and the result of that course. Notice first, the course of action. *"He that covers his sin."*

To "cover" sin means, literally, to smooth it over. To cover sin would be similar to "plumping up" a feather mattress, comforter or pillow. To "cover up" means to make the appearance different from reality. When we cover up our sin, we hide the truth; we disguise our true spiritual condition.

The result of covered sin is that we *"will not prosper."* Here, "prospering" means to make progress or to push ahead. There are six reasons why a person who covers his sin will not go forward in his home, his work, or his relationship with God.

1.) Covered sin is an evidence of pride. We are reminded in James 4:6 that *"God resists the proud, but gives grace to the humble."* Many people say they are reluctant to confess the sin in their life because "they don't want to hurt the one they love." But the truth is, in most cases, a refusal to confess reveals an unwillingness to become humble before God and others. God always resists, or stiff-arms the proud.

The first eleven verses of Proverbs 26 reveal God's opinion of the fool. These verses are an indictment against a person who turns from God and the wisdom of God's Word and operates only on the basis of his knowledge or desire. You cannot read these verses without realizing how despised a fool is in the eyes of both God and man. However, verse 12 tells us, *"Do you see a man wise in his own eyes? There is more hope for a fool than for him"*

(Proverbs 26:12). Pride reduces a person below the level of folly. And covered sin is evidence of pride.

2.) Covered sin manifests itself in rebellion. *"The wicked flee when no one pursues: but the righteous are bold as a lion" (Proverbs 28:1).* Children often wonder how parents can sense when there is a problem in their life. Parents can usually tell when something's wrong because often, a child's covered sin will manifest itself in a rebellious attitude. The son or daughter who says, "Get off my back!" in response to the simple question, "Did you have a good time this evening?" is, more than likely, covering sin. Also, people who will not humble themselves, but instead try to cover sin, ultimately begin to defend sin in the lives of other people. But the person who is truly humble, seeing himself as God sees him, realizes there is nothing to be gained by covering sin.

3.) Covered sin destroys the "completeness" in your relationship with God and others. A person who is covering sin must constantly maintain a wall around that sin. The closer people get to the wall, the higher they must build it. Sometimes, a married person will say, "What my partner doesn't know can't hurt." Yet a partner can usually sense when sin is being covered. He or she may not know the details, but they know that something is wrong. This develops a lost sense of completeness in the relationship. It is as if you are saying, "There is a part of my life you will never have the opportunity to examine."

4.) Covered sin removes the ability of others to protect you from temptation. The Scriptures tell us to *"...consider one another in order to stir up love and good works"* (Hebrews 10:24). One of the ways we can encourage one another in love and good works is by establishing accountability in our relationships. This means that others will have the privilege of asking us serious questions about our life and our lifestyle. But when we refuse to humble ourselves and we continue to cover sin, accountability is lost, because those to whom we should be accountable have no way of knowing the areas in which we are experiencing our greatest temptations. God has placed people in our lives to encourage us, and yet we often refuse to allow them to see the areas of our greatest struggles.

5.) Covered sin leads to a greater possibility of repetition because we do not see the destructive and hurtful results of our disobedience. It would be wise for us to remember the experience of David when he sought to cover the sin he committed with Bathsheba. Until he was confronted with his sin and was willing to humble himself in confession and repentance, David was caught in a spiral of disobedience which led himself and others into more sin and even murder. Furthermore, people who cover their sin often think that it will not hurt to get more deeply involved because, after all, they haven't gotten caught so far, and therefore, they could probably indulge more without being discovered.

6.) Covered sin robs the person against whom you sin of the privilege of growing in the Godly grace of forgiveness. Just as God is working to conform you to His image, He is also working in the lives of others. One of the most Godly of all characteristics is the quality of forgiveness. If you will humble yourself and confess your sin, God will not only grant grace to you, but He will give the person against whom you've sinned the grace to forgive. This could be a great step of maturity in their spiritual pilgrimage.

Is it any wonder that our refusal to humble ourselves and confess our sin and our persistence in covering sins has such a damaging effect upon our lives, our relationship with others, and most importantly, our relationship with God.

II. THE CLEAR CORRECTION
"Whoever confesses and forsakes them will have mercy."

Once again, the Scripture presents both the course of action and the result of that course. First, there is a two-fold course of action.

1) We are to confess our sin. This means we must say about our sin what God says about our sin. This is ultimately an act of deep humility and contrition. We are to confess to God because all sin is against Him. (This is why David's confession began with, *"Against You, You only, have I sinned, and done this evil in Your sight..."* (Psalm 51:4).) But then, we must also confess to the individual(s) against whom we've sinned. A confession should be as wide, but only as wide, as the circle of our offense. If we have only offended one person, we only need to confess to that person. If we have offended the entire church, we should confess to the entire church.

When we're asking someone's forgiveness, our confession should be complete. *"If we say that we have fellowship with Him, and walk in darkness, we lie and do not practice the truth. But if we walk in the light as He is in the light, we have fellowship one with another, and the blood of Jesus Christ His Son cleanses us from all sin"* (1 John 1:6-7).

Pride produces a confession which is incomplete, but humility "covers all the bases." Failure to be complete in our confession will breed a lack of trust on the part of others. I have known some people, for instance, who began to confess, but when they saw the hurt in the heart of the one to whom they were confessing, they stopped short of confessing everything. Even when asked, "Is that all?" they replied, "Yes, that's all I need to confess." But they have just backed up their garbage truck, tilted it a little so that only part of the garbage fell out, and then lowered it and driven off, still carrying around the garbage of unconfessed sin in their heart. As God continues to convict them, they bring the truck back again, dump out a little more of their spiritual garbage at the feet of the offended party, and once again say, "That's all there is." After two or three experiences like that, most people begin to seriously doubt whether the individual is being honest. True humility breeds **complete** confession.

2) Then there is the importance of repentance as it relates to confession. In the New Testament, repentance means a change of heart that results in a change of action. In this particular passage, repentance also means to loosen, or relinquish your grip on something; to forsake. There is a sense in which we have not repented of any sin that we are still committing. Repentance means that you close all the doors, behind you and ahead of you, through which any temptation can come to draw you back into that sin. Repentance means that by the grace of God, your heart's desire is to relinquish any attachment to that sin.

Finally, notice the result of following this course of action. *"You will have mercy."* Certainly, there will be mercy from God; and in most cases, you will receive mercy from those against whom you have sinned. What a wonderful result comes from following the clear correction as opposed to the costly cover-up!

Do you remember the three people I described at the beginning of this chapter? While they are fictional characters, their struggles represent the deep feelings of many people. We could write an ending to their stories which would either show them continuing to hide their sin or properly dealing with it. Suffice it to say that if that pastor, seminary student, and husband would humble themselves, God would grant His mercy, and they would begin to prosper spiritually. *"He who covers his sins will not prosper." "If my people, who are called by my name, will humble themselves..."* This is revival's first step.

9

A Quiet Place,
A Quiet Time

"...and pray..."

"When Jesus had spoken these words, He went out with His disciples over the Brook Kidron, where there was a garden, which He and His disciples entered. And Judas, who betrayed Him, also knew the place; for Jesus often met there with His disciples" (John 18:1-2).

Jesus made it clear that the central issue in lordship is obedience. *"But why do you call me 'Lord, Lord,' and do not do the things which I say"* (Luke 6:46)? And again, *"Not everyone who says to me, 'Lord, Lord,' shall enter into the kingdom of Heaven, but he who does the will of my Father in Heaven"* (Matthew 7:21). But if there is an area where we fail most often to obey the precepts of Christ, it is the arena of prayer. By both example and exhortation, He constantly reminded us *"...that men always ought to pray and not lose heart..."* (Luke 18:1).

The scene portrayed in the text above is as revealing as it is touching. Our Lord is with His disciples on the eve of His crucifixion. They have observed the Feast of the Passover together and now, crossing over the Brook Kidron, they enter the garden of Gethsemane. Judas has already arranged his betrayal of Christ, and now he makes his way through the streets of Jerusalem, followed by a cohort of Roman soldiers. (It is estimated that there were between 300 and 600 Roman soldiers with Judas that evening.) It is worth noting that Judas did not have to lead these soldiers on a "wild goose chase" through the streets of Jerusalem looking for Jesus. Judas knew where Jesus could be found. For Jesus, *"...often met there with His disciples."* Judas knew Jesus would be in His place of prayer.

In your life, do you have a quiet place and a quiet time where consistently, day by day, you spend time in prayer with the Lord? Is that place and time so firmly established that, as in the case of Jesus, or in the case of Daniel, years earlier, a plot for your life could be built upon the common knowledge that at a specific time, you could be found praying in a specific place. On the following pages, you will discover the benefits of having a quiet place where you spend a quiet time with the Lord on a consistent basis.

I. IT WILL BE A PLACE AND TIME OF COMMUNION WITH THE FATHER

Mark's gospel reveals that during His Gethsemane experience, Jesus entered into a time of intimate communion with the Father.

> *"Then they came to a place which was named Gethsemane; and He said to His disciples, 'Sit here while I pray.' And He took Peter, James, and John with Him, and He began to be troubled and deeply distressed. Then He said to them, 'My soul is exceedingly sorrowful, even to death. Stay here and watch.' He went a little farther, and fell on the ground, and prayed that if it were possible, the hour might pass from Him. And He said, 'Abba, Father, all things are possible for You. Take this cup away from Me; nevertheless, not what I will, but what You will'"* (Mark 14:32-36).

Note particularly the expression "Abba, Father." As mentioned in Chapter 6, the term "abba" is a phrase of tender endearment. Unlike the more formal word "father," its equivalent in our culture would be "daddy." This is the kind of intimate communion with the Father that can only be developed through a consistent prayer life.

I have two observations regarding the result of communion with the Father. First, it is folly to seek counsel from people who do not seek counsel, themselves, from God. We have a tendency to divide our lives into the secular and the spiritual. Secular matters might include our finances, or perhaps our vocation. Spiritual matters have to do with our relationship with the Lord. In seeking counsel regarding secular matters, we normally don't consider the spiritual depth of the person from whom we seek counsel. I know of many Christians, for instance, who seek counsel regarding their finances from some of the most godless sources. On the other hand, they feel that it would be only appropriate to seek counsel regarding spiritual matters from people who are spiritual minded.

But God does not make an artificial division between the secular and the spiritual. Our entire life is to be a spiritual offering unto Him. This means that when we seek counsel, whatever the issue, we should consult people who appreciate the counsel which comes from God through His Word.

My wife once scheduled an appointment with our children's pediatrician to ask specific questions about his personal relationship with Christ. He was surprised she asked. For one reason, he just assumed she knew he was a church member, but also he didn't see any relationship between his spiritual life and his ability to be a good physician for our children. My wife told him that she did indeed know that he was a church member, but since he would be counseling with her regarding the welfare of our children, she wanted to know more about his relationship with the Lord. In particular, she was interested in knowing just how often he sought the counsel of the Lord regarding his patients!

It is not only important for us to seek counsel from those who seek counsel from the Lord, but it is equally important for us *not* to give counsel to others unless we have sought the counsel of the Lord. Sometimes, I think we respond to people's questions with a careless "knee-jerk" attitude. Often with little thought or prayer, we tell them "what we would do about the situation." It is important for us to hear from God before dispensing advice to others.

After thirty years of pastoral counseling, I became discouraged when I realized that there were just a few people who demanded a majority of my counseling time, and these same people seemed to make very little progress. I then realized how little prayer and thought I was giving to their problems. This brought about a significant change in my counseling style. Instead of giving immediate advice, I began to ask more questions about their situation and would then say, "Now that I have a grasp of the problems you are facing, I want to pray over this matter and seek the counsel of God through the Scriptures. When He gives me leadership, I will call you and share with you what He has shared with me." The results of this type of counseling amazed me. I noticed that those whom I counseled placed a greater value on the words I shared, and when they followed my advice, their lives were changed for the better. The difference was obvious: I was seeking the counsel of God before giving counsel to others. My new approach to counseling required that I spend more time in prayer each day.

A quiet place where you spend a quiet time will be a place and a time of intimate communion with God.

II. IT WILL BE A PLACE AND TIME OF CONFLICT

It could be that the greatest struggle surrounding Christ's crucifixion took place, not on the cross, but in the garden of Gethsemane. Look at Dr. Luke's vivid account of the physical struggle which took place in the garden:

> *"Coming out, He went to the Mount of Olives, as He was accustomed, and His disciples also followed Him. When He came to the place, He said to them, 'Pray that you may not enter into temptation.' And He was withdrawn from them about a*

stone's throw, and He knelt down and prayed, saying, 'Father, if it is Your will, remove this cup from Me; nevertheless not My will, but Yours, be done.' Then an angel appeared to Him from Heaven, strengthening Him. And being in agony, He prayed more earnestly. And His sweat became like great drops of blood falling down to the ground" (Luke 22:39-44).

Jesus was experiencing "hematidrosis," a physiological condition in which the capillary action of the blood changes to the extent that clots of blood emerge through the pores of one's body. It occurs in people who are under severe stress. This was a time of immense struggle for our Lord. Jesus knew that He would soon be arrested and falsely accused; His beard would be pulled from His battered and bruised face; a crown of thorns would pierce His scalp and scrape against His skull. Professional "scourgers" would beat Him with strips of leather imbedded with pieces of metal and glass. They would literally "beat Him within an inch of His life"; a practice which frequently left visceral organs exposed through gaping wounds in the body. Then Jesus, after carrying His cross to Golgotha, would be stretched out upon it, and heavy spikes would be driven through His extremities. His bones would be ripped out of their sockets as the cross was lifted up and suddenly dropped into the socket prepared in the ground.

Crucifixion was the most excruciating means of execution ever devised by sinful man. If the person did not die from infection, or loss of blood, he would gradually drown in the fluids of his own body. Able to inhale but not exhale, the chest cavity would gradually fill up with fluid. That explains why blood mixed with water flowed from the wound when the soldier pierced Jesus' side.

And Calvary was not a beautiful green hill. It was a filthy, foul smelling place where the dogs prowled, the worms crawled, the flies swarmed, the crowd jeered, and the others being crucified screamed.

In vivid contrast to all of the confusion which surrounded the crucifixion, Jesus exhibited great self-control. He never "flew off the handle;" He never lost His composure. While the sins of the world were placed upon Him, He brought order to the moment and only died when He chose to do so.

In like manner, no believer's life is without conflict. It is part of the growth process. Someone has written:

> When God wants to drill a man and skill a man and thrill a man; when God wants to mold a man to play the noblest part, and when He yearns with all His heart to create so great and bold a man that all the world shall be amazed, watch His method, watch His ways, how He ruthlessly perfects whom He royally elects. How He hammers him and hurts him and with mighty blows converts him into trial shapes of clay which only God understands and his tortured heart is crying and he lifts beseeching hands how, He bends but never breaks whom his good He undertakes. How He uses whom He chooses and with every purpose fuses him and by every act induces him to try His splendor out. God knows what He's about.
>
> --Angela Morgan (adapted)

Conflict is inescapable in your life. People who maintain calm in the midst of conflict shine like bright stars against a horizon of chaos. But who are these people who can be calm in the midst of conflict? I believe they are the people who settle their conflicts in their quiet time. When asked the secret of a successful, long-term ministry, E. F. "Preacher" Hallock, then pastor of First Baptist Church of Norman, Oklahoma, responded with these words, "Fight every battle on your knees."

Some people are under the misconception that conflict always indicates that you are out of God's will. But that is certainly not the case. Moses would rarely have won a popularity contest - he went from one conflict to another; and yet, with few exceptions, he was always in the center of God's will as he led the children of Israel out of Egypt to the border of the Promised Land. During His earthly ministry, even Jesus was frequently opposed. It was conflict which ultimately led to the cross.

It's exciting to realize, however, that many conflicts may be hammered out on the anvil of your life in the confines of your prayer closet. From there, you can step forward to meet the enemy head on with the knowledge that victory is assured.

III. IT WILL BE A PLACE AND A TIME OF CONFORMITY TO THE WILL OF GOD

Matthew's record of the Gethsemane experience says:

> *"He went a little farther and fell on His face, and prayed, saying, 'O My Father, if it is possible, let this cup pass from Me; nevertheless, not as I will, but as You will.' Then He came to the disciples and found them asleep, and said to Peter, 'What? Could you not watch with Me one hour? Watch and pray, lest you enter into temptation. The spirit indeed is willing, but the flesh is weak.' He went away again a second time and prayed, saying, 'O My Father, if this cup cannot pass away from Me unless I drink it, Your will be done.' And He came and found them asleep again, for their eyes were heavy. So He left them, went away again, and prayed the third time, saying the same words" (Matthew 26:39-44).*

It appears that there was a great wrestling match going on in the garden of Gethsemane that night. Knowing that the cross was before Him, Christ's humanity wrestled against that which was divine. It was not an easy battle. Our Lord's statement, *"The spirit indeed is willing, but the flesh is weak,"* is most likely a reference to the fact that that which was of the flesh was crying out against the agony of the cross, while that which was spiritual responded by saying, *"Nevertheless, not as I will, but as You will."* It was not until there was total conformity to the will of God that our Lord came to His disciples and said, *"Behold, the hour is at hand, and the Son of Man is being betrayed into the hands of sinners."*

From the moment of our conversion, God has one basic purpose for all of our lives during our earthly journey: He wants to conform us to the image of His Son. And that conformity can occur during our quiet times with Him. Sadly, many of God's children allow so little time for conformity in the quiet place that God is forced to deal with them in the public arena. As an example, we are reminded that humility is one of the most noted characteristics of Christ. If we will not humble ourselves before God during that quiet hour, He will be forced to humiliate us publicly. One way or the other, we will learn humility.

I have a friend who calls me occasionally to ask if the Lord has shown me "some new thing." I usually don't look forward to those calls, but on one occasion I was ready with an answer. "I have learned how to get all I want!" I replied. He responded with surprise, "That sounds rather crass, cold, and commercial." "I know it does," I responded, "but it's true, nonetheless." Here is the truth I shared with him, **"If I could just get to the place in my life where all I wanted for my life was simply all that God wanted for my life, then all of my life, I would have all I wanted, and He would have all of me He wanted!"** The key, of course, is getting to the place where "all we want is all He wants for us." This is the essence of conforming to His will.

The longer I live, the more convinced I am that the greatest work of God in the heart of man can take place in the prayer closet where we spend our quiet time with Him.

Communion, conflict, conformity. All of these essentials await you in that quiet place where you spend your quiet time with the Lord. May it be know of us that, like our Lord, there is a place where we often resort to meet Him.*

*For a study of these same characteristics in the life of Moses, read the author's book, The Pathway To God's Presence, Nashville: Broadman Press, 1990 pp. 53-59.

10

What Will You Find In the Face of God?

"...and seek my face..."

"When you said, 'Seek My face', my heart said to You, 'Your face, Lord, I will seek,'" (Psalm 27:8).

A terrible thunderstorm was sweeping across the plains and into the Texas town where I was serving as pastor during my seminary days. As lightning raced across the sky and thunder cracked directly overhead, our young daughter, sleeping in the next room, cried out in fear. I hurried to her bedside and sought to encourage and comfort her. But my words failed. "Lie down here beside me, Daddy," she pleaded. And so I eased into the bed beside her and lay there staring at the ceiling. As the thunder and lightning continued, my daughter's fears seemed to grow in spite of all that I could say. Then she asked a very simple question: "Daddy, is your face toward me?" I rolled over on my side, facing her, and said, "Yes, sweetheart, my face is toward you." With that, her restlessness ceased, and it seemed only a matter of seconds before her heavy breathing indicated that she was sound asleep in the midst of the storm, confident that she was safe because her father's face was toward her.

In our revival text, 2 Chronicles 7:14, we are told that in addition to humility, prayer, and repentance, we should seek the face of God. Like David, our response should be, "Thy face, Lord, will I seek." But what will you find in the face of God?

I. GOD'S FACE REGISTERS HIS ACCEPTANCE

It is interesting how the countenance of close friends and family members register the answer to this question: "Are you for me or against me?" Similarly, as we seek the face of God, we are searching for His acceptance.

One of the great comforting thoughts which every believer should cherish is the knowledge that God is "for" His children. *"For I know the thoughts that I think toward you, says the Lord, thoughts of peace and not of evil, to give you a future and a hope"* (Jeremiah 29:11).

When I was growing up, one of the things I appreciated most about my parents was the fact that my friends were always welcome in our home. Though my parents were always gracious and polite to everyone I invited home, I could quickly sense, simply by watching their countenance, whether or not they felt the relationship would be healthy or destructive for their son. It was not so much what they said as it was what I sensed by examining their demeanor. Since I knew they loved me and only wanted what was best for me, I was always eager to develop the friendships of which they approved.

I remember when someone explained to me what a "poker face" meant; it is a face you can't "read," which supposedly is of great value in a card game. But our Lord is never "poker faced" with His children. He never leaves us guessing about our relationship with Him. He wants us to know that even though He may disapprove of some of our activities, He is still for us and wants only the best for us. When you look into His face, you will find His acceptance. The Apostle Paul tells us that because of our relationship with the Father, through Christ, *"...He has made us accepted in the Beloved"* (Ephesians 1:6).

Some years ago, my wife was giving a stern rebuke to one of our children. The longer she talked, the more impressed she was with the keen interest our child was giving her. As a matter of fact, that child's eyes were riveted to my wife's eyes. She finally asked, "Do you understand my concern?" Our child's answer revealed the reason she was looking so intently, "You know, Mommy, when I look real hard, I can see me in your eyes!" She saw her image reflected in her mother's eyes. When you look closely in the face of God, you can see "you" in His eyes. You are accepted as His child.

II. GOD'S FACE REFLECTS HIS ATTENTION

We can often discover what a person is interested in by following his gaze, by noticing the focus of his attention. One of the chief aims of every believer is to find the Lord's focus of attention so that we might cooperate with His plan.

I remember observing a young couple sitting near me at a football game. It soon became obvious that they were totally absorbed in each other! The football game was, apparently, only an excuse to be together. They were oblivious to the players on the field and the spectators in the grandstand. They literally "only had eyes" for one another. By observing their faces, I could easily tell the object of their attention. Similarly, we discover God's interests by seeking His face.

One of the great secrets to success in the Christian life is finding God's focus and then aggressively cooperating with Him in that work. Many years ago, revivalist Manly Beasley came to speak at a church where I had just begun a new pastorate. He would call me several times during each day and ask a simple question: "Tom, what is your heart's desire?" I don't remember all of the answers I gave him, but I once answered, "My heart's desire is to grow a great church." On another occasion, I stated that "My heart's desire is to see many people come to know

Christ." All of my answers seemed quite noble to me, but they never seemed to satisfy Brother Manley.

Toward the end of the week, God did a deep work in my own heart, and I realized that there was only one good answer. When Manly Beasley called Friday afternoon to ask that same question, "What is your heart's great desire?" I blurted out, "To know Christ!" "Praise God!" he responded, "Now, maybe revival will come!" And come it did! God moved in might and power: hearts were stirred, lives were changed, and interestingly enough, a great moving in our church was born. Manly Beasley's initial concern was that my attention, my focus of interest, was not the same as the Lord's - that's why he was not satisfied with my other answers. Only when I began *to seek His face*, did I discover God's goal for my life and for our church, and then His interest became my interest.

III. GOD'S FACE REGISTERS HIS ATTITUDE

When our four children were very young, we would often take them to the beach or to a pool. I knew that I would hear these words hundreds of times over during the next several hours: "Daddy! Daddy! Watch this!" My children were wanting my attention, but they were also searching for something more - my approval. They wanted to know what I thought of what they were doing.

It is not enough for us just to know that God accepts us as His children. Nor is it enough just to know where God's attention is focused. We must seek the face of God in order to discover His *attitude,* that is, His approval or disapproval of our activities and the intents of our hearts. Notice the importance of God's face in the benediction God gave to Aaron and to his sons through Moses.

"Speak to Aaron and his sons, saying, 'This is the way you shall bless the children of Israel. Say to them:

> *"The Lord bless you and keep you; the Lord make His face shine upon you, and be gracious to you; the Lord lift up His countenance upon you, and give you peace. "'*
>
> *So they shall put My name on the children of Israel, and I will bless them" (Numbers 6:23-27).*

It's also interesting to note that God is looking at *our* face, because the intents of our hearts are often reflected in our countenance. Our countenance often speaks more loudly than our words. 2 Chronicles 7:15 states, *"Now My eyes will be open and My ears attentive to prayer made in this place. "* In other words, God is saying, "I am not only listening to what you say, I am watching what you do!" If He is so attentive to our behavior, we should likewise look to His face in order to discover His attitudes.

IV. THERE IS ASSIMILATION IN THE FACE OF GOD

Most people are familiar with the legend of "The Great Stone Face." Up on the side of a mountain, overlooking a city, there seemed to be etched in stone, the face of a noble man. In the town below, one man in particular would often gaze upon that great stone face and reflect upon the enduring, honorable characteristics which he imagined that the face portrayed. Over the years, not only did he adopt those qualities as his own, but the people in his town noticed that he began to take on the actual appearance of the great stone face. His life was changed as he contemplated and emulated the noble image.

In like manner, I have noticed that the longer a husband and wife live together and love each other, the more they begin to take on each others' appearance and mannerisms. They develop a similarity in their love, their laughter, their language, and even in their looks. As in the instance of the great stone face, they have assimilated those qualities they admire in each other.

When we intently seek the face of God and consider Him the object of our love, we will become like Him. Our Lord, for instance, states that as we follow Him, He will make us to become what He is, *"fishers of men"* (Mark 1:17). Moses, after he met with the Lord on Mount Sinai, left with a glowing countenance which was a reflection of the Shekinah glory of God (Exodus 34:35). Paul reminds us that his magnificent obsession was *"that I may know Him and the power of His resurrection, and the fellowship of His sufferings, being conformed to His death..."* (Philippians 3:10). The process of conforming is the kind of assimilation which occurs as we seek the face of our Lord.

Humility and prayer prepare us to seek the face of God. And in the act of seeking, we discover acceptance, attention, attitude, and assimilation. It is then that we are moved to turn from our wicked ways. As you seek revival, it is legitimate to ask, "What have I found in the face of God?"

11

No Repentance...
No Revival

"...and turn from their wicked ways..."

"If My people who are called by My name will humble themselves, and pray and seek My face, and turn from their wicked ways, then I will hear from Heaven, and will forgive their sin and heal their land. Now My eyes will be open and My ears attentive to prayer made in this place" (2 Chronicles 7:14-15).

What started out as the "annual scheduled revival" on the seminary campus became **genuine** revival when God hijacked the first chapel service. In the days that followed, the Holy Spirit brought deep conviction of sin to both students and faculty. Students confessed to their professors that they had not been totally honest on reading assignments and tests. Professors confessed to professional jealousy and competitiveness. In response to an awesome wave of His power, we were moved first to confession and then to repentance. In the end, God brought wonderful restoration, affecting first the atmosphere of the campus, then spilling over into the homes and churches of students and faculty.

At the very heart of genuine revival is repentance of sin. We readily acknowledge the necessity of repentance in salvation because repentance is turning from sin. But our experience of salvation is to be the pattern for the balance of our Christian life.

"As ye have therefore received Christ Jesus the Lord, so walk in Him..." (Colossians 2:6). And since repentance was a fundamental aspect of our salvation experience, it must play an important part in our daily walk with Christ. Sin drives a wedge in our fellowship with God; therefore, it must be confessed and rejected if our fellowship is to be restored.

I. THE REALITY OF SIN IN THE BELIEVER'S LIFE

In our text, God insists that His people, called by His name, should humbly and prayerfully seek His face. But in order to do so, they must *"turn from their wicked ways."*

The Bible is clear on the fact that God's people are not immune to sin. Our struggle with sin is so real that the Bible pictures us as combatants in the arena of faith. Consider the lives of these great men of faith. Noah, whose faith caused him to be the one man enlisted to provide a remnant after the flood, fell into sin after that great deliverance. Abraham, the great man of faith, was not impervious to sin; his ill-fated journey to Egypt produced a relationship out of which were born a people who continually strived with God's people. Moses, the heroic and faithful leader of Israel, brought them to the border of the Promised Land but was not permitted to enter in himself because of sin. And consider David, the man after God's own heart. His "secret sin" has been known to the world for over 2,000 years.

Listen to the heart-rending lament of the Apostle Paul:

> *"For I know that in me (that is, in my flesh) nothing good dwells; for to will is present with me, but how to perform what is good I do not find. For the good that I will to do, I do not do; but the evil that I will not to do, that I practice. Now if I do what I will not to do, it is no longer I who do it, but sin that dwells in me. I find then a law, that evil is present with me, the one who wills to do good. For I delight in the law of God according to the inward man. But I see another law in my members, warring against the law of my mind, and bringing me*

*into captivity to the law of sin which is in my members. O
wretched man that I am! Who will deliver me from this body of
death? I thank God - through Jesus Christ our Lord! So then,
with the mind I myself serve the law of God, but with the flesh
the law of sin"* (Romans 7:18-25).

Paul was obviously no stranger to sin.

In the first epistle of John, the believer is confronted with the
reality of sin in his life:

> *"If we say that we have no sin, we deceive ourselves, and
> the truth is not in us. If we confess our sins, He is faithful and
> just to forgive us our sins and to cleanse us from all
> unrighteousness. If we say that we have not sinned, we make
> Him a liar, and His word is not in us. My little children, these
> things I write to you, so that you may not sin. And if anyone
> sins, we have an Advocate with the Father, Jesus Christ the
> righteous. And He Himself is the propitiation for our sins, and
> not for ours only but also for the whole world"* (1 John 1:8-
> 2:2).

The point is obvious: believers struggle with the reality of sin.
Personal revival will only come when you acknowledge that sin
has disturbed and diminished the quality of your relationship with
the Savior.

II. THE REPULSIVENESS OF SIN IN
THE BELIEVER'S LIFE

In our text, God says restoration is directly related to our
willingness to see the wickedness of sin as God sees it. Sin is
repulsive to God. He cannot look upon any sin with the least
degree of allowance.

> *"But the wicked are like the troubled sea, when it cannot
> rest, whose waters cast up mire and dirt. There is no peace,
> says My God, for the wicked"* (Isaiah 57:20-21).

But while the sin of the lost world is repulsive to God, the sins of His people are even more so.

For instance, imagine a man who, after a beautiful time of courtship, finally rejoices in the privilege of taking his beloved as his wife. She becomes the focus of his love, the object of his affection. He lives for her, and he sacrifices all for her. When he is away from her, his thoughts are still upon the great joy it is to have her as his wife. She is on his mind and heart night and day. He always carries her picture and frequently takes it out to look at and proudly show others how blessed he is to have her as his wife. There is no request she could make but that he would bend Heaven and earth to fulfill it. She is the great love of his life.

But what this faithful and dedicated man does not know is that secretly, through the years of their courtship and now their marriage, she is a practicing prostitute. Shortly after he leaves for work in the morning, she slips out of the house; and during the day, while he is dreaming of her, she is in one adulterous bed after another. While he remains faithful to her, she has lost count of her lovers. Imagine the heart-breaking discovery that awaits him.

In like manner, we have played the harlot with the lover of our souls. The church is the bride of Christ; He died for her and now lives for her. His heart's great desire is that she may be presented, one day before the Father, pure and holy in her radiant, righteous apparel. But she is a prostitute, and God knows it. Her sinful affections and dalliances with the world pierce His heart moment by moment and will continue to do so until one day He calls His bride home to Heaven. How repulsive our sin must be to our Savior.

The brokenness that attends revival comes when God's people begin to see sin as God sees it and acknowledge its awfulness. Historically, in the beginning days of great revival movements, there was not the song of joy so much as the weeping of repentance. Believers who are on the verge of revival are usually found on their faces, crying out before the Lord over the repulsiveness of sin in their lives. Notice that one of the marks of true conversion is that the believer will not continue committing the same sins in the same way because he has been born of God (see 1 John 3:6-9).

III. THE RESPONSE OF GOD TO SIN IN THE BELIEVER'S LIFE

The Scriptures indicate that God deals with sin in the believer's life through a series of three progressive steps: conviction, chastening, and, finally, the call home or "the sin unto death."

God's first response to our sin is to bring **conviction** to our heart. His Holy Spirit employs the Word of God which is *"living, and powerful, and sharper than any two-edged sword, piercing even to the division of soul and spirit, and of joints and marrow, and is a discerner of the thoughts and intents of the heart"* (Hebrews 4:12). Through His Word, and by His Spirit, God speaks to our hearts about the sin in our lives. Just as a mirror shows us the way we look to others, so the Word of God shows us the way we look to Him. The Holy Spirit uses the Word much like a sailor uses a compass. As we read the Bible, we become aware that we have strayed from the course He has charted for our lives.

But suppose we make no correction of course? Suppose we ignore the Spirit's voice and do not confess and repent of our sin? God then begins to **chasten** us.

> *"And you have forgotten the exhortation which speaks to you as to sons:*
> *'My son, do not despise the chastening of the Lord, nor be discouraged when you are rebuked by Him; for whom the Lord loves He chastens, and scourges every son whom He receives.'*
> *If you endure chastening, God deals with you as with sons; for what son is there whom a father does not chasten? But if you are without chastening, of which all have become partakers, then you are illegitimate and not sons. Furthermore, we have had human fathers who corrected us, and we paid them respect. Shall we not much more readily be in subjection to the Father of spirits and live? For they indeed for a few days chastened us as*

seemed best to them, but He for our profit, that we may be partakers of His holiness. Now no chastening seems to be joyful for the present, but grievous; nevertheless, afterward it yields the peaceable fruit of righteousness to those who have been trained by it" (Hebrews 12:5-11).

As noted in the Scripture, chastening is so common for a believer that the failure to experience it, as God's response to persistent sin, clearly indicates that an individual is not even a child of God.

What happens if God's child does not respond to conviction or chastisement? It is then possible that God would **call the believer home**. 1 John 5:16 speaks of the sin unto death. The sin unto death is not so much a specific sin (such as adultery or murder). It is, instead, a specific kind of attitude toward sin. It is a high-handed alacrity regarding sin; the deliberate choice to persist in sin in spite of conviction and chastisement. Basically, its saying that you are so confident of your relationship with the Father, that you are willing to presume upon His love by continuing to engage in the very thing which is so repulsive to Him. If a believer continues to ignore God's voice and chastisement, he could reap the judgement of Luke 13:9, *"And if it bears fruit, well. But if not, after that you can cut it down."*

David referred to presumptuous sin as the "great transgression." Listen to his plea: *"Keep back Your servant also from presumptuous sins; let them not have dominion over me. Then I shall be blameless, and I shall be innocent of great transgression"* (Psalm 19:13). We should remember that although David sinned greatly, when confronted by the prophet of God, his heart melted and his spirit was broken.

God is committed to deal with our sin. He may do it through conviction, chastening, or death. But it is important to realize that God is searching for repentance on our part. He wants us to repent so that we can return to Him, come back to His table, and experience restored fellowship with the Father.

IV. THE RESTORATION AVAILABLE TO THE BELIEVER WHO SINS

Our text holds within it the great promise of restored fellowship with God - the promise that He will hear, forgive, and heal our land. It is remarkable that, in spite of our sin, God would have any desire at all to keep the way open for fellowship with Him. It is an evidence of His long-suffering and His grace.

The promise of restoration is preceded by six conditions: salvation (if my people), external evidence through Christ-like behavior (which are called by My name), genuine humility (shall humble themselves), earnest prayer (and pray), an intense search for the heart of God (and seek My face), and repentance (and turn from their wicked ways). These conditions for restoration in no way diminish the fact that revival, ultimately, is a sovereign work of God. It simply means that God, in His sovereignty, is disposed to move toward those whose lives exhibit these characteristics.

A coach can place any team member he chooses out on the field, but in making that choice, he will be predisposed to use those players who have diligently conditioned themselves for competition. Similarly, if we desire revival, we must realize that it is a sovereign work of God, but at the same time, we should earnestly strive to fulfill the conditions presented in this passage.

Note also the character of this restoration. It is three-fold: God first states that He will hear the plea of our heart. Since we know that God has repeatedly illustrated His desire that we fellowship with Him, we can say that revival is His will for us. Believing it is His will, we may then claim the following promise: *"Now this is the confidence that we have in Him, that if we ask anything according to His will, He hears us. And if we know that He hears us, whatever we ask, we know that we have the petitions that we have asked of Him"* (1 John 5:14-15). Secondly, God will forgive our sin: *"If we confess our sins, He is faithful and just to forgive us our sins and to cleanse us from all unrighteousness"* (1 John 1:9).

And finally, He promises to heal our land. Many times, when speaking of the "sickness" of our nation, we are, in reality, only speaking of the symptoms. When the Lord heals our land, He moves straight to the cause of those symptoms, brings cleansing by His blood, and restores fellowship. Speaking to sinful Israel, God urges, *"Come now, and let us reason together, says the Lord, though your sins are like scarlet, they shall be as white as snow; though they are red like crimson, they shall be as wool. If you are willing and obedient, you shall eat the good of the land; but if you refuse and rebel, you shall be devoured by the sword; for the mouth of the Lord has spoken"* (Isaiah 1:18-20).

A closing word: God calls us to restoration: *"Now My eyes will be open, and My ears attentive to the prayer made in this place"* (2 Chronicles 7:15). In essence, the Lord is saying, "Here are the conditions of restoration. Here is the character of that restoration. Now I have called you to restoration. It's your next move." I have a friend who has said to me on more than one occasion, "If God is silent, it's your next move! The ball is in your court."

Repentance is the hinge upon which revival turns. It is both a prerequisite for revival and an evidence of genuine revival. In essence: No repentance...No revival!

Notes

1. John H. Evans, *AFA Journal,* May 1992, p. 21.
2. Michael Medvid, "Popular Culture and War Against Standards," *Imprimis*, February 1991, p. 1.
3. Ibid., p. 1.
4. "Childhood," published by Family Research Council, p. 70.
5. Ibid., p. 70.
6. Ibid., p. 69.
7. From a letter written by Robert G. DeMoss, Jr., of Focus on the Family, July 7, 1992.
8. Michael Medvid, "Popular Culture and War Against Standards," *Imprimis*, February 1991, p. 3.
9. Thomas Jipplin, J.D., "Garbage In, Garbage Out: Children, Music, and Responsibility for Culture," *Policy Insights*, published by Free Congress Foundation, April 1992, p. 2.
10. Ibid., p. 2.
11. As quoted in a letter written by James Dobson of Focus on the Family, June 1992.
12. Mona Charen, "Illegitimacy Latest Fad for Television Writers," *The Daily Oklahoman,* October 2, 1991, p. 6.
13. As quoted in "Childhood," published by Family Research Council, p. 68.
14. *T.V.* Guide, August 22-28, 1992, p. 10-11.
15. For a detailed study, see the chapter "A Pornographic Nightmare," in David Hocking's book, *The Moral Catastrophe,* Harvest House Publishers, 1990.
16. From the video "Fatal Addiction," from Focus on the Family.
17. Kenneth Woodward, "The Elite, and How to Avoid It," *Newsweek*, July 20, 1992, p. 55.
18. L. Lichter, R. Lichter, and S. Rothman, "Hollywood and America: The Odd Couple," *Public Opinion*, Dec/Jan 1983, p. 55.
19. Kenneth Woodward, "The Elite, and How to Avoid It," *Newsweek,* July 20, 1992, p. 55.
20. Thomas Jipplin, J.D., "Garbage In, Garbage Out: Children, Music, and Responsibility for Culture," *Policy Insights*, published by Free Congress Foundation, April 1992, p. 2.
21. Ibid., p.1.
22. From an article, "Does Morality Save Hollywood?" by Bob Pierce.

Chapter Two

1. As quoted in a letter to Gary Bauer, Family News In Focus broadcast, July 1, 1991.

2. From "The Church's Response to the Challenge of AIDS/HIV," MAP International, P.O. Box 50, Brunswick, GA, 31521.

3. From figures released in 1992 during an International Congress on AIDS.

4. Larry Thompson, "The AIDS Statistics," *Washington Post.*

5. From "Impacting the Legacy of AIDS," published by Americans for a Sound AIDS/HIV Policy, P.O. Box 17433, Washington, D.C., 20041.

6. Dr. Lorraine Day, *AIDS: What the Government Isn't Telling You.* (Palm Desert, CA: Rockford Press, 1991).

7. Joe McErhaney, Jr., "Safe Sex - A Doctor Explains the Reality of AIDs and Other STDs."

8. Dr. Lorraine Day, *AIDS: What the Government Isn't Telling You.* (Palm Desert, CA: Rockford Press, 1991).

9. From "The Church's Response to the Challenge of AIDS/HIV," MAP International, P.O. Box 50, Brunswick, GA, 31521.

10. From "Washington Watch," published by Family Research Council, January 1992.

11. From "Safe Sex for Teens," published by ACT UP, Oklahoma City.

12. From "Condom Roulette," by Gary Bauer, of Family Research Council.

13. In subsequent press conferences, Magic Johnson has admitted that the only safe sex is no sex outside of marriage.

14. Letter published in *The Arkansas Citizen*, January 1992.

15. Robert C. Noble, "There is No Safe Sex," *Newsweek*, April 1, 1991.

16. See "Sexual Disorientation," for an excellent study on the errors of the highly touted Kinsey report, published by the Family Research Council.

17. Dr. Lorraine Day, *AIDS: What the Government Isn't Telling You.* (Palm Desert, CA: Rockford Press, 1991).

18. Tom Hess, "They Call This Abstinence," *Citizen*, published by Focus on the Family.

Chapter Three

1. David Hocking, *The Moral Catastrophe*, p. 32.

2. Carol Everett, *The Scarlet Lady - Confessions of a Successful Abortionist*, p. 162.

3. Ibid.

4. *Newsweek*, August 17, 1992.

5. David Hocking, *The Moral Catastrophe,* p. 32.

6. Carol Everett, *The Scarlet Lady - Confessions of a Successful Abortionist.*

7. "Abortion: Is There a Health Risk?" In Focus, Family Research Council, June 1991.

8. Ibid.

9. Nancy Mann, *Where Does Life Begin?*

10. Mark Crutcher, "Abortion Questions They'd Rather Duck," *Citizen*, published by Focus on the Family, May 20, 1991.

Chapter 4

1. An excellent study of their decision is available from: Christian Advocates Serving Evangelism, P.O. Box 450349, Atlanta, GA, 30345.

2. As quoted in David Barton's, *The Myth of Seperation.*

3. Ibid.

4. Ibid.

5. From a letter written by James Dobson of Focus on the Family, June 1992.

6. As quoted in David Barton's, *The Myth of Separation.*

7. David Barton, *America: To Pray or Not To Pray,* (Aleda, TX: Wallbuilder Press, 1988, 1991).

8. As quoted in the "Student's Bill of Rights." Copies may be obtained by calling or writing the publisher: Roever Communicators, PO Box 136130, Fort Worth, Texas, 76136, 817-237-2587.

Other Books Available from NCM Press:

The Pathway to God's Presence - Tom Elliff - $8.95
> Chapters include: When the Glory is Gone From Your Life, The Vital Signs of God's Presence, Going On in the Glory Of God, The Sinister Side of Success.

Praying For Others - Tom Elliff - $5.95
> Chapters include: The Practice of Prayer, The Biblical Method of Intercession, The Danger of Not Getting a Word From God, Why Prayers Are Hindered.

The Practice of Praise: A Manual For Worship Renewal
Don McMinn - $8.95
> Chapters include: The Priority of Worship, The Praise Transition, The One Who Worships, Observable Elements of a Praise and Worship Service.

Strategic Living: How To Set And Accomplish Goals
Don McMinn - $7.95
> Chapters include: Do It! - How To Accomplish Goals, Excuse Me, I'm Busy - Becoming Efficient, Who Pushed Me? - Motivation.

Order all books from: NCM Press
                        2104 Banbury
                        Oklahoma City, Oklahoma, 73170
Sales Tax: Please add 7.375% for books shipped to
             Oklahoma addresses
Shipping: $1.50 for the first book, add 50 cents
             for each additional book.
Payment required with all orders.
Make checks payable to NCM Press